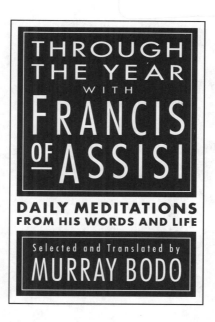

THROUGH THE YEAR
W I T H
FRANCIS OF ASSISI

DAILY MEDITATIONS
FROM HIS WORDS AND LIFE

Selected and Translated by
MURRAY BODO

ST.
ANTHONY
MESSENGER
PRESS

CINCINNATI, OHIO

Cover design by Julie Lonneman
Cover illustration by George Hardebeck

Illustrations copyright ©1987 by Doubleday & Company, Inc.

ISBN 0-86716-196-5

©1993, Murray Bodo

Published by arrangement with Doubleday, a division of Bantam
Doubleday Dell Publishing Group, Inc. All rights reserved.

Published by St. Anthony Messenger Press
Printed in the U.S.A.

For Roch and Aaron,
my pilgrim brothers in St. Francis

A Portrait of St. Francis

He was quite an eloquent man, with a cheerful and kindly face. He was without cowardice or insolence. He was less than medium in height, bordering on shortness. His head was of moderate size and round, his face somewhat long and striking, with a smooth, low forehead. His eyes were black and clear and of average size; his hair was black and his eyebrows straight, his symmetrical nose was thin and straight. His small ears stood up straight and his temples were smooth. His speech was peaceable, but fiery and crisp; his voice was strong, sweet, clear, and sonorous. His teeth were closely fitted, even, and white; his lips were small and thin; his beard was black and not bushy. He had a slender neck, straight shoulders, short arms, slender hands with long fingers and extended nails; his legs were thin, his feet small. He had delicate skin and was quite thin. He wore rough garments, slept sparingly, gave most generously. And because he was very humble, he showed mildness to everyone, adapting himself to the behavior of all. Among the holy he was even more so; among sinners he was one of them.

—Celano, First Life, 83

Introduction

1

I have been on a spiritual journey to and with St. Francis since my thirteenth year, and most of the selections in this book were made on actual pilgrimages to Assisi. Therefore what I say here in this introduction and the daily entries themselves are after the manner of a notebook from a pilgrim who has drawn on the words of St. Francis to guide him on life's way.

The way of pilgrimage is the way of death leading to life. You leave behind loved ones and home, entrusting their safety and care to God, who is drawing you away from them. It is God who leads the pilgrim as he leads the dying person, and you follow shyly, awkwardly, fearfully, at first; then letting go somewhere along the way, you surrender what you've left behind into the very hand that is clasping yours on the journey.

An image of all this rises in my mind, a poem by the German poet Rainer Maria Rilke entitled "The Swan":

> This laboring through what is still undone,
> as though, legs bound, we hobbled along the way,
> is like the awkward walking of the swan.
>
> And dying—to let go, no longer feel
> the solid ground we stand on every day—
> is like his anxious letting himself fall
>
> into the water, which receives him gently
> and which, as though with reverence and joy,
> draws back past him in streams on either side;
> while, infinitely silent and aware,
> in his full majesty and ever more
> indifferent, he condescends to glide.*

* *The Selected Poetry of Rainer Maria Rilke,* edited and translated by Stephen Mitchell, New York: Random House, 1982, p. 29.

It is not so much where you are going as the going away, the leaving itself, that matters. It is consigning to God what you thought was so dependent on your presence: your loved ones, your affairs. You leave, not knowing for certain that you will return. You embark upon a journey of faith, from faith to faith.

It is not that one place on earth is more in God's hearing than another, so that he hears me better "there" than "here." But it is what happens to my own hearing in traveling "there" to listen, when the things and people of "here" begin to speak too loudly for me to hear my own inner voices and the voice of the Spirit.

In the Middle Ages those who went on pilgrimage wondered if they would ever return; the slowness of the journey and the dangers along the way made reaching one's destination doubtful. Today the pace is faster—jet travel, telephone communication with one's loved ones back home—realities that make our pilgrimage seem less radical, less drastic a decision than it was in ages past. And in one sense that is true.

In another sense, however, nothing has changed. There is still the decision to set forth on one's own in the company of strangers, in order to lay one's ear, opened along the way, against the mouth of God that spoke once in the place or through the person whose shrine we are drawn to.

And somehow we go alone, even if we are in the company of others, even of our loved ones. For our journey is largely made in the heart (perhaps from the mind to the heart), an inner rather than an outer journey. The outer journey can indeed be made with others; the inner cannot, though perhaps the words of someone living or dead may make our journey seem less solitary.

And so it has been and is, that I bring with me on all my travels the words of St. Francis. They are food for the journey because most of them were written or spoken for those who are "on the road," so to speak, mendicants, beggars who travel two by two throughout the world, though inwardly they are hermits, because, as St. Francis says, they carry their cell with them. He envisions the brothers as pilgrims on the road, and what he says is like practical advice for those who are constantly leaving something or someone behind.

Unlike the usual idea of a pilgrim, however, St. Francis's conception is not of someone going to a place made holy by others; rather, it is of those who make every place holy in their going there. His words are a way of making holy the journey to anywhere. His words sanctify the way.

As we journey through life, we not only leave something behind, but we gain something as well. Like Rilke's swan, "infinitely silent and aware," in "full majesty and ever more indifferent," we "condescend to glide."

In essence, that is what the words of St. Francis, when put into practice, enable us to do. And it is God in whom we glide so easily, the God we feared, the God we perhaps did not think was there anymore as we labored out of our element like swans on land looking for water.

We learn that the water is there, that it is not so frightening as we thought, that if we let go, we will begin to glide easily, gracefully, to where we one day will remain forever. Pilgrimage is a testing of the waters of eternity. And the words of St. Francis make that testing less frightening; they make it, in fact, exciting. In the spoken and written experience of St. Francis we discover someone who lives comfortably in the waters of eternity, even while on earth.

There is always in the pilgrim's way the way of the penitent. For as we embark upon a journey to God, we are immediately aware of how far we really are from him for whom we long, toward whom we are journeying. That is the main reason why the words of St. Francis sound at times rather negative, rather deprecatory of what is earthly, even of what is human.

He is not saying that the body, the world, the human person are evil. He is only saying that apart from God, without God, in comparison to God, we and everything else that exists are really nothing. Of ourselves we are worthless and vile. Of *ourselves,* on our own, as it were.

9

St. Francis's viewpoint is that of someone whose journey has led him into another dimension, the world of the Spirit, which completes and makes intelligible all that is. He sees the whole picture and is therefore unimpressed with the works and deeds of humankind. He sees human beings in the total scheme of things—how insignificant they really are compared to the Most High, Omnipotent, Good God, who alone is Good, who alone is God.

We who live for the most part on the human level find it hard to stomach some of the things St. Francis says, because we tend to affirm and celebrate only what is thoroughly human: human goodness, human dignity, human worth. All of which is valid and good—until you move into that other world within our world, the world of God's Spirit. For you cannot experience that world by human effort, or goodness. Only God can take you there, and his leading you begins with an experience of conversion which humbles you before the Good God, an experience which opens up for you the infinite chasm between Creator and creature.

Nor is this just a medieval point of view, a regression to another age, a slipping back into superstition and ignorance. This experience that changes, transforms the person, is ancient and medieval and modern; yesterday, today, and tomorrow. It is an experience of the living God and it leaves one breathless with wonder, burdened with one's own unworthiness. It is the experience of Isaiah the Prophet:

In the year of King Uzziah's death I saw the Lord seated on a high and lofty throne; his train filled the sanctuary. Above him stood seraphs, each one with six wings: two to cover its face, two to cover its feet and two for flying; and they were shouting these words to each other:

"Holy, holy, holy is Yahweh Sabaoth.
His glory fills the whole earth."

The door-posts shook at the sound of their shouting, and the Temple was full of smoke. Then I said:

"Woe is me! I am lost,
for I am a man of unclean lips
and I live among a people of unclean lips,
and my eyes have seen the King, Yahweh
Sabaoth."

(Is 6:1–6)

It is this awareness of his unworthiness before so good and great a God that inspires St. Francis to say and write things which, taken out of context, may seem Puritanical, or, to locate it in his own time, Albigensian, that heretical stance which sees matter as evil and spirit as good and never the twain to meet.

Nothing could be further from what St. Francis really believed. His was an incredible awareness of the Incarnation and what that meant. The Word had become flesh. Spirit and matter had conjoined irrevocably in Jesus Christ. To denigrate matter is to say that Jesus Christ is tainted with something evil; it is to be anti-sacramental, and St. Francis was the supremely sacramental man, wholly Catholic, wholly eucharistic in his spirituality.

So when St. Francis says something negative about us humans, we need to place it in the context of his total vision, and we can do this by mentally adding this phrase to whatever negative statement he makes: "in comparison to God, apart from God."

What transcends the material is infinitely above it, rendering the natural vile and worthless in comparison. In other words St. Francis's negativity toward the finite, the material, the temporary, is always juxtaposed to what is infinite, supernatural, eternal. His vision includes both, and so he is constantly penitent, repentant when he finds himself and others overvaluing the material, the human, and devaluing the spirit.

Another way of saying this would be: There is only one perfect human being, Jesus Christ, the eternal Incarnation of Spirit. It is only in him and through him and with him that we live and move and have our being, and we make ourselves wretched and vile when we fail to see and live this truth. And this then is sin, to keep preventing the incarnation of spirit

11

within us, to keep trying to kill God, crucifying Jesus over and over again. That is what we can claim as our own, St. Francis says, and not grace, which is God's work alone.

St. Francis, like all great poets, brings the world inside himself and there imagines it, images it. But unlike some poets, St. Francis's inside is not emptiness, dread, absence. It is radiant with the light of God, imaged as the splendor of the sun become our Brother, Jesus Christ.

Brother Sun (Son) lights up the whole world of images in the soul of St. Francis. There is no darkness except in the decision to refuse the light. In that we are wretched and vile and unworthy, for light is there if we but open the lids of our soul.

In some strange and wonderful way St. Francis's complete servitude was his freedom. Like a medieval craftsman, subservient to the architect's design, yet making his own gargoyles, he managed to carve out, in subservience to God, the sculpture of a life uniquely his own. And not only to God was he obedient, but to every living creature as well. And he encouraged his brothers and sisters to do the same, knowing that only in obedience would they become uniquely who they were.

How can this be? Doesn't this kind of obedience make automatons of us all? If it did, then we would not be able to distinguish one saint from another. But, of course, we can distinguish them, and saints are among the most unique, easily distinguishable personalities in history.

The reason, in St. Francis's case, at least, is because he is obedient not in a compulsive, detailed way, but to the overall scheme. It is to the vision that St. Francis is obedient, not to the mechanical, unthinking execution of compulsions. Furthermore, it is a vision not of the mind but of the heart and results from the way of love rather than the way of knowing.

2

Much of what St. Francis wrote and said is by way of admonition and instruction of his brothers and sisters. His inspiration, as he himself says, is what the Lord himself has told him and what he has heard proclaimed from Sacred Scripture. He listened to the Lord wherever he heard his word; and meditating upon this word, he put it into practice. As Francis himself says, "No one showed me what I was to do, but he, the Most High, revealed to me that I was to live according to the form of the Holy Gospel" (The Testament). And, "Every day I find so much sweetness and consolation in meditating upon the memory of the humble witness of the Son of God, that should I live till the end of the world, there would be little need of my hearing or meditating upon anything further in the Scriptures" (Legend of Perugia, 99).

What we find in the writings and sayings of St. Francis is often the kind of thing we find in the exhortations of St. Paul, or more pointedly in passages like this one from St. James, whose shrine, at Compostela in Spain, Francis visited on pilgrimage, as did so many devout Christians of the Middle Ages:

> Where do these wars and battles between yourselves first start? Is it not precisely in the desires fighting inside your own selves? You want something and you lack it; so you kill. You have an ambition that you cannot satisfy; so you fight to get your way by force. It is because you do not pray that you do not receive; when you do pray and do not receive, it is because you prayed wrongly, wanting to indulge your passions.
>
> Adulterers! Do you not realize that love for the world is hatred for God? Anyone who chooses the world for a friend is constituted an enemy of God. Can you not see the point of the saying in scripture, 'The longing of the spirit he sent to dwell in us is a jealous longing'? But he

has given us an even greater grace, as scripture says: 'God opposes the proud but he accords his favor to the humble.' Give in to God, then; resist the devil, and he will run away from you. The nearer you go to God, the nearer God will come to you. Clean your hands, you sinners, and clear your minds, you waverers. Appreciate your wretchedness, and weep for it in misery. Your laughter must be turned to grief, your happiness to gloom. Humble yourselves before the Lord and he will lift you up.

(Jm 4:1–10)

We would do well to remember this Scripture passage if we continue to be surprised at what the joy-filled Saint of Assisi sometimes says. St. Francis's attitudes are not merely those of a simple, saintly, but unenlightened man of the Middle Ages who has little to say to the liberated modern world. St. Francis is the total Gospel person, hearing the Good News proclaimed and interpreted in the liturgy of the Church. He does not rationalize or explain away any of the words of the Lord. He simply hears them and puts them into practice. This was what was called "devotion" in the Middle Ages: alacrity in putting into practice the word of God.

But like the Gospel itself, the words of St. Francis can only be understood in the context of full Gospel living, of a life lived wholly in and by the word of God. Outside of that total vision (and vision is what it is) the admonitions of St. Francis, and of St. James for that matter, are indeed at times "unenlightened" and could even be misleading. What then is that vision, what is the Gospel life as it was revealed to St. Francis?

It seems to me that the key to Francis's vision is that he experiences the transcendent, all-holy God while he is still in his sins, so that he is intensely aware of God's goodness and holiness and, simultaneously, of his own sinfulness as a human being, as one of those who lost the gift of paradise through their own fault. Therefore, repentance-and-penance, not only for his own sins but for the sinfulness of humankind, is a constant, recurring motif in the life of St. Francis. It is not that he is always bemoaning his unworthiness and sinfulness in a

14

self-pitying way, but the holiness and goodness of God and our ingratitude for the bounty he pours out upon us makes Francis aware of our sinfulness and unworthiness, our need to be purer vessels for holding all that God is lavishly pouring into us.

How we are to do this is revealed to Francis through the Holy Gospel, and so he sets out to live the words he hears in the Gospel; and this is the life of penance he preaches about and tries to live. To live the Gospel literally is what makes one a more fitting vessel for the outpouring of God's gifts. Furthermore, to live the Gospel is to walk in the footsteps of Jesus Christ whose incarnation, passion, and death is the supreme penance, the Most High himself becoming Most Low: "Make your own the mind of Christ Jesus:

> Who, being in the form of God,
> did not count equality with God
> something to be grasped.
>
> But he emptied himself,
> taking the form of a slave,
> becoming as human beings are;
>
> and being in every way like a human being,
> he was humbler yet,
> even to accepting death, death on a cross."

(Ph 2:5–8)

So when we empty ourselves and become most low, we participate in the life and death of Jesus Christ, the only penance that really counts, the penance our small penances participate in when we do them out of love for him who did his great penance out of love for the Father and us.

3

There is something archetypal about St. Francis, something that rises from deep within us when we meet him, something we find in Assisi itself. It walks the streets unseen, it comes invisibly around corners wearing a fiery cloak that fans the air like the wings of seraphs hot with God.

What is this something, and why do so many feel it rising within them as they pass through the gates of a medieval mountain town whose very name is a variation of the old Italian word "ascesi," which means, "I have risen"? Dante says it is Francis himself, who, like the sun, rose upon the earth and was still a mere dawn when we began to feel the warmth and light his rising brought us:

> Therefore, whoever seeks to name this place
> should not say, "Assisi." That would not do it.
> Rather say, "The Rising," to name what happened there.

> For the sun wasn't long in its rising
> when he began to warm and lighten the earth
> with the comfort of his great power.

(*Paradiso,* Canto XI)

St. Bonaventure develops this theme of light and says that what really rises in us is the realization that

> God's grace has been revealed
> in his servant Francis
> to all who are truly humble, truly friends of holy
> poverty . . .

> He was a little poor one, contrite of heart
> but God looked kindly upon him . . .
> and raised him up as a *light* for believers
> so that by bearing witness to the *light*

he might prepare in the hearts of the faithful
a way of *light* and peace for the Lord.

(Major Life of St. Francis, Prologue)

This is mystical, symbolic language, and yet we glimpse its
truth, we feel its pull upon the heart, even if we don't fully
understand all that is being said. Dante and St. Bonaventure
are both writing in the power of medieval mystical theology,
which may seem far removed from us moderns in our post-
Freudian, atomic age, us moderns who have split the atom and
the psyche and don't know how to put them back together. Is
there, then, a way of saying what Dante and Bonaventure say
so profoundly that will define more clearly for us what it is that
rises in us when we come face to face with the mystical, be it in
a place or a person?

Perhaps we can begin with that very word, "mystical," which
has its roots in the word "mystery," whose oldest Greek root
means to close the lips or eyes. What is it that we see or hear
when we do close our lips or eyes? In that profound gesture is
contained the beginning of an understanding (modern or ancient, or medieval), of that seemingly dark center out of which
we experience that rising in the soul which we cannot name.
And, yes, I've used another word here, "soul," that some
moderns shudder at, preferring "psyche," which incidentally
means soul in Greek, but which in English has a rather cold,
clinical sound to it with all kinds of dark, frightening over-
tones. Is not "soul" a better word for that mystery within,
which we keep running from by refusing it anything other than
a clinical, scientifically analyzable reality? Carl Jung says:

> People will do anything, no matter how absurd, in order
> to avoid facing their own souls. They will practice Indian
> yoga and all its exercises, observe a strict regimen of diet,
> learn theosophy by heart, or mechanically repeat mystic
> texts from the literature of the whole world—all because
> they cannot get on with themselves and have not the
> slightest faith that anything useful could ever come out of

17

their own souls. Thus the soul has gradually been turned into a Nazareth from which nothing good can come.*

But something good does come from Nazareth, and so I close my eyes and lips and pray in that secret place called soul, waiting for him to come who is Son, and for him to raise me up who is Father. And therein begins all mystical experience: in waiting for God, in the freedom of his love, to come and love me, instead of doing frantically all sorts of things to "make" him love me. I keep trying to prove I'm good by doing, giving, thereby preempting God, not letting him come to me first, not receiving. And I do this because I am afraid he really does not love me as the beautiful work of his own loins, but only if I *win* his love.

The so-called *Peace Prayer of St. Francis* has the line, "It is in giving that we receive," but that can only be prayed well by one who knows that it is only "in receiving that we give." For God has first loved us, and given himself to us, and that is what we learn from the mystics like St. Francis, who are brave enough to close their eyes and lips and listen. Then what begins to rise in us is that which has been lifted up by him who comes in love, and what he lifts up is the heart itself, rising from within to meet the Love descending to embrace it.

This is what I've learned in Assisi, in the unhurried land of Umbria, from St. Francis, who in summer gave of himself in compassion to others on the road, but in winter returned to the mountaintop and entered the cave of the closed eyes and lips, and waited. Had he remained on the road, his giving would only have been to prove to himself that he was as good as his good works proclaimed he was. Had he remained always in the cave, blind and silent, he would only have proved his own self-absorption instead of that meeting with him who raises up and draws out the heart to follow him down the

* *Psychology and Alchemy*, second edition, par. 126, quoted in *C. G. Jung, Psychological Reflections, A New Anthology of His Writings, 1905–1961*, edited by Jolande Jacobi and R. F. C. Hull, Bollingen Series, XXXI, Princeton University Press, 1970.

mountain where he summers in those his embrace has led us to embrace.

This, too, then I have learned. And these pages are the words of him who taught it to me, of him who learned the lesson and the words by closing his eyes and lips and waiting. These are the words St. Francis spoke after that prayer which is a closing of eyes and lips to pray to one's Father in secret. These are the words I've heard wherever or whenever I read the words of Francis with my own eyes closed and my own lips sealed.

January
St. Francis and His Brothers

January 1

A New Kind of Fool

The Lord has called me into the way of simplicity and humility, and he has indeed made this way known through me and through all who choose to believe me and follow me. So I prefer you not talk to me about any other Rule, whether St. Benedict's, or St. Augustine's, or St. Bernard's, nor recommend any other ideal or manner of life than that which the Lord in his mercy has revealed and given to me. He told me I am to be a new kind of fool in this world.

—Mirror of Perfection, 68

January 2

St. Francis Speaks of the Early Days of the Brotherhood

This is how our brothers lived in the early days at the Portiuncula, the church of Our Lady of the Angels. Although it was already a holy place, they made it even more holy by constant prayer and silence. If anyone spoke after the time set aside for silence, it was to speak devoutly and discreetly of things pertaining to the praise of God and the salvation of souls.

They curbed the desires of the flesh, not only by fasting, but also by frequent vigils, by enduring the cold in light clothing, and by working with their hands. In order to avoid idleness, they would often go and help poor farmers work their fields, and sometimes after work the farmers would share their bread

23

with them for the love of God. They sanctified themselves and the place by these and other virtuous acts.

—Legend of Perugia, 57f

January 3

St. Francis's Advice to a Minister*

Let there be no brother who has sinned, no matter how seriously, who would look into your eyes seeking forgiveness, and go away without it. And should he not seek forgiveness, you should ask him if he wants it. And if after that he were to sin a thousand times, even before your eyes, love him more than me, for this is how you will draw him to the Lord; and always have mercy on such as these.

—Letter to a Minister

January 4

The Rule of the Lesser Brothers

NOTE: St. Francis calls his friars, or brothers, "lesser," to locate them in society among the little people, the poor and lowly, who were called "minores," "lesser ones," in medieval Italy. The more affluent, or the nobility, were called "majores," or "greater ones."

In the name of the Lord begins the Life of the Lesser Brothers! The Rule and Life of the Lesser Brothers is this: to observe

* "Minister" is a superior, a word that St. Francis does not use for those brothers in positions of authority.

24

the Holy Gospel of our Lord Jesus Christ by living in obedience, without anything of their own, and in chastity.

—Rule of 1223, Chapter I

January 5

Concerning Preachers

You should not preach in the diocese of any bishop who has forbidden you to do so. And you should not dare preach to the people unless you have first been examined and approved by the minister general of this brotherhood, who officially confers the office of preaching.

I also admonish and exhort those who preach to use well-chosen and chaste words that are practical and edifying. And let them point out to the faithful what is evil and what is virtuous, what merits punishment and what leads to eternal glory. And let your discourse be brief, because the Lord's words were few when he was on earth.

—Rule of 1223, Chapter IX

January 6

The Spirit of the Lord and His Grace

Guard against all pride, vanity, envy, avarice, the cares and worries of this world, detraction and complaining. And if you do not have book-learning, do not be eager to acquire it, but pursue instead what you should desire above all else, namely, to have the Spirit of the Lord and his grace working in you, to pray always with purity of heart and to have humility, patience in persecution and in infirmity, and to love those who persecute and rebuke and slander you, because the Lord says, "Love your enemies and pray for those who persecute you" (Mt 5:44). "Blessed are those who are persecuted in the cause of uprightness: the kingdom of Heaven is theirs" (Mt 5:10). "Anyone who stands firm to the end will be saved" (Mt 10:22).

—Rule of 1223, Chapter X

January 7

Of Those Who Are Sick

I ask the sick that in everything you give thanks to the Creator. And whatever it might be that the Lord wants for you, whether it be health or sickness, let that be what you want also. For all those the Lord has "destined for eternal life" (Acts 13:49) he teaches by using the allurement of trials and sickness and compunction of spirit. As the Lord himself says, "I reprove and train those whom I love" (Rv 3:19). And if you become upset or angry either against God or against others, or are overly insistent on medicines to free the flesh which is soon to die anyway and is the enemy of the soul, that kind of behavior comes from the evil one. It is carnal and is not seemly because it shows that you love your body more than your soul.

—Rule of 1221, Chapter X

January 8

Lesser Brothers

Francis, the model of humility, wanted his brothers to be called Lesser and the superiors of the Order to bear the name "servants," thereby preserving the very words used in the Gospel which he had promised to observe. At the same time he enabled his followers to learn from their very name that they had come to the school of the humble Christ to learn humility. Jesus Christ, the teacher of humility, intending to form his disciples in true humility, said, "Anyone who wants to become great among you must be your servant, and anyone who wants to be first among you must be your slave" (Mt 20:26–27).

—St. Bonaventure, Major Life, 6:5

January 9

Make Your Needs Known to One Another

Be confident in making your needs known to one another. For each of you, to the extent that God gives you the grace, should love and nourish one another as a mother loves and nourishes her child.

—Rule of 1221, Chapter IX

January 10

St. Francis's Natural Courtesy

Even before his conversion St. Francis was by nature courteous in manner and speech and followed a practice born of deep conviction, namely, never to speak a rude or unseemly word.

—Legend of the Three Companions, I, 3

January 11

The Lowest of Sinners

St. Francis was the humblest of men and thought of himself as the lowest, most contemptible of sinners. In prayer he would implore, "Lord, why have you laid this burden on me? Why have you made a simple, unlettered, wretched creature like me the head of this Order?" And the Lord would reply, "I have placed a man like you over this Order to show that what I achieve in you is of my grace and not a human accomplishment."

—From a sermon of St. Bonaventure, October 4, 1262

January 12

St. Francis's Portrait of the True Franciscan

St. Francis used to say that a good Lesser Brother should emulate and possess the virtues of these holy brothers: "Brother Bernard's perfect faith and love of poverty; Brother Leo's simplicity and purity, Leo, that man of such holy purity; Brother Angelo's courtesy, the first nobleman to enter the Order, a man who was all courtesy and kindness; the gracious bearing and common sense of Brother Masseo, and his noble and devout eloquence; a mind lifted up to God, which Brother Giles possessed in the highest degree; the constant prayer of Brother Rufino, who, asleep or waking, seemed always to be praying, his mind ever fixed on God; the patience of Brother Juniper, who attained the state of perfect patience by keeping the truth of his low estate constantly before him and whose supreme desire was to follow Christ on the way of the cross; the physical and spiritual courage of Brother John of Lauds, who in his day was physically stronger than everyone; the charity of Brother Roger, whose every deed and word was inspired by fervent charity; the caution of Brother Lucidus, who wouldn't stay in any place more than a month, for when he began to like a place, he would leave immediately, saying, 'Our home is not here, but in heaven.' "

—Mirror of Perfection, 85

January 13

St. Francis Educates St. Anthony

I am pleased that you are teaching sacred theology to the brothers, so long as this kind of study, as our Rule has it, does not extinguish the spirit of prayer and devotion.

—St. Francis's Letter to St. Anthony

January 14

St. Francis Receives Brother Giles into the Order

Eight days after the first two companions, Brother Bernard and Brother Peter, were received into the Order, Brother Giles was received by Francis at the Portiuncula. He was a fellow Assisian, a man full of faith and devotion to whom the Lord had given a singular grace. On his knees, and with great devotion and reverence, he begged Francis to receive him into their family. And the saint, pleased with what he saw and the words he heard, received him gladly. Then these first four brothers experienced an extraordinary spiritual joy.

Years later St. Francis said of Brother Giles that he more than any other had arrived at the perfection of contemplative prayer. And Brother Giles himself used to say, "The contemplative life is to leave behind all earthly things for the love of God, to seek only the things of heaven, to pray without tiring, to read often and with concentration, to praise God continually with hymns and canticles. To contemplate is to be separated from all and to be united to God alone."

—The Anonymous of Perugia, Chapter 3, #14;
The Mirror of Perfection, 85; The Golden Sayings of
Brother Giles, Chapter XIII

January 15

Overcoming Shame

And when people shame you by refusing you alms, you should give thanks to God for that, because in recompense for shame we receive great honor before the judgment seat of our Lord Jesus Christ. And you should know that shame is imputed not to the one who suffers it, but to the one who inflicts it. And alms are the inheritance and the justice due the poor which our Lord Jesus Christ acquired for us. You who labor to acquire alms, then, have a great reward and also enrich those who give to you; for everything that people leave behind in the world will perish, but for the charity and almsgiving they've practiced they will have their reward from the Lord.

—Rule of 1221, Chapter IX

January 16

The Marvelous Companions of St. Francis

Just as the holy Apostles were marvels of holiness and humility throughout the whole world, and were filled with the Holy Spirit, so the companions of St. Francis were of such sanctity that not since the time of the Apostles were there such marvelous and holy men in the world. It happened that one of them was caught up into the third heaven as St. Paul was, and this was Brother Giles. Another, namely Brother Philip Lungo, had his lips touched by an angel with a burning coal as did Isaiah the prophet. Another, Brother Sylvester, spoke with God as one friend to another, as Moses did. Another, with subtlety of intellect, flew like the Eagle, John the Evangelist, all the way into the light of Divine Wisdom, and that was Brother Bernard, the humble one, he who opened up the Scriptures in the most profound ways. Another was sanctified by God and canonized in heaven even while he lived on earth, and that was Brother Rufino, a true gentleman of Assisi.

—Little Flowers of St. Francis, Chapter 1

January 17

A Message of Peace

St. Francis used to say to his brothers, "Go, announce peace to all people; preach repentance for the remission of sins. Be patient in trials, watchful in prayer, and steadfast in weariness. Be modest in your speech, responsible in your actions, and grateful to your benefactors. And know that in return an eternal kingdom is being made ready for you."

—St. Bonaventure, Major Life, 3:7

January 18

Obedience

Among other graces which the Divine Mercy has deigned to give me is this: If a novice only one hour in the Order were made my guardian,* I would obey him as scrupulously as I would the oldest and most prudent brother in the Order. A subject should not see the man in the prelate,* but him for whose love he is subject.

—St. Bonaventure, Major Life, 6:4

January 19

Those Who Wish to Join the Brotherhood

If anyone by divine inspiration wishes to embrace this life and comes to our brothers, let him be kindly received by them. And if he remains constant in his resolve to accept our life, the brothers are to be careful not to meddle in his temporal affairs, but they are to present him as soon as possible to their own minister. Let the minister receive him kindly and encourage him and diligently explain to him the nature of our life. After this, if he is willing and able to do it in conscience and is without legal impediments, he is to sell whatever he has and set about giving the sum to the poor.

—Rule of 1221, Chapter II

* "Guardian" and "prelate" are words for religious superiors.

January 20

St. Francis's Care for His Sick Brothers

It happened once that a sick brother longed to eat just a few grapes. So St. Francis took him by the arm to a vineyard, and sitting with the sick brother beneath some vines, Francis began to eat first, to give the brother courage to eat too.

—Celano, Second Life, 176

January 21

The Preaching and Example of St. Francis

My office of governing the brothers is spiritual, in that I must overcome and correct vices. If I cannot do this by my preaching and example, then I surely do not want to do it like a taskmaster, beating and flogging the brothers the way a worldly master does.

—Writings of Leo, Rufino, and Angelo, 23b

January 22

On Those Brothers Who Are Placed in Authority

"The Son of man came not to be served but to serve" (Mt 20: 28), says the Lord.

Those brothers who are placed in authority over the others are to glory in their office as much as if they were appointed to wash the feet of the brothers; and if they are more disturbed when their office is taken from them than they would be if the service of washing feet were taken from them, then to that extent have they amassed treasures for themselves to the peril of their souls.

—Admonition 4

January 23

St. Francis's Love and Affection for a Troubled Brother

One day Francis said to Brother Riccerio, who was deeply troubled interiorly: "Don't let your thoughts depress you, for you are very dear to me. Know that you are among those especially dear to me and worthy of my affection and intimacy. Come to me confidently whenever you wish, and don't be afraid to talk to me with utmost familiarity."

—Celano, First Life, 50

January 24

A Holy Contract

There is a contract between the world and the brothers: The brothers are bound to give the world a good example, and the world to provide for their necessities. If, then, the brothers break their contract by reneging on their good example, the world will withdraw its hand in just censure.

—Celano, Second Life, 70

January 25

A Letter for Brother Leo

Brother Leo, wish your Brother Francis health and peace! I want to say this, my son, as a mother would. My response to all the words we spoke along the way I would sum up in a brief counsel; and should you wish to come to me later for my advice, this is what I would say: Whatever seems best to you in order to serve the Lord God and to follow his footsteps and his poverty, do it with the blessing of the Lord God and with the blessing of my obedience. And if you believe it is necessary for the good of your soul or for your consolation to come to me, and you want to come, then, Leo, do come!

—Parchment written by the hand of Francis himself.
It is kept in the Cathedral of Spoleto, Italy.

January 26

St. Francis's Words on Working

I used to work with my hands, as I still want to, and I want all the other brothers to work at a task which is honest and becoming to our manner of life.

Those who do not know how to work should learn, not because they are eager for the pay due their labor, but for example's sake and to banish idleness. And when we receive no pay for our work, let us have recourse to the table of the Lord, begging alms from door to door.

—The Testament of St. Francis

January 27

Of Brother Bernard of Quintavalle

Brother Bernard was the first brother the Lord gave me. He was the very first to begin and to fulfill the perfection of the Holy Gospel by distributing all his goods to the poor. For this reason and for the many other good qualities in him, I am bound to love him more than any brother of the whole Order.

—Writings of Leo, Rufino, and Angelo, 42

January 28

Conformity to Christ

In everything he did, St. Francis was conformed to Christ.
When he began his Order, he did as the Blessed Christ had
done when he chose twelve Apostles to despise the things of
this world and follow him in poverty and the other virtues. He
too had twelve chosen companions who were followers of total
poverty.

—Little Flowers of St. Francis, Chapter 1

January 29

How the Early Brothers Lived

We prayed the Office, the clerics like other clerics, and the laics
saying their Our Fathers. And we most willingly lived in abandoned churches. And we were without learning and subject to
all.

—The Testament of St. Francis

January 30

The Beginnings of the Order of St. Francis

And after the Lord gave me some brothers, no one showed me what to do; but the Most High revealed to me that I was to live according to the manner of the Holy Gospel. And I had it written down in brief, simple words, and the Lord Pope confirmed it for me.

And those who came to receive this life gave everything they had to the poor; and they were happy with one tunic patched inside and out, and with a cord and breeches.

And we had no desire for anything else.

—The Testament of St. Francis

January 31

Admonition for Peacemakers

The peace which you proclaim with words must dwell even more abundantly in your hearts. Do not provoke others to anger or give scandal. Rather, let your gentleness draw them to peace, goodness, and concord. This is our vocation: to heal wounds, to bind what is broken, to bring home those who are lost.

—Legend of the Three Companions, 58

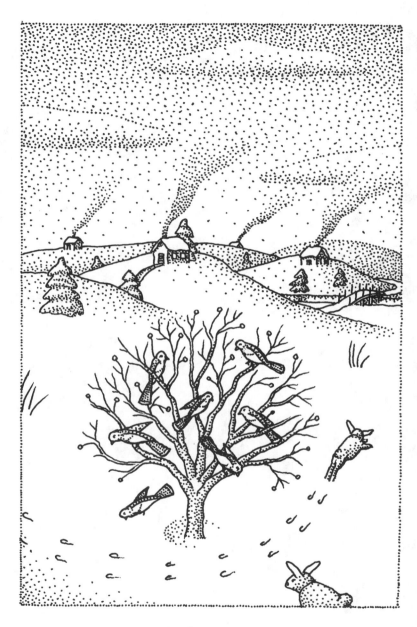

February

Lady Poverty

February 1

Hearing the Gospel on the Feast of St. Matthias, 1208

One day at the very beginning of his conversion, St. Francis was attending Mass at the Portiuncula, and he heard the priest proclaim the words of Christ whereby he sends out his disciples to preach and admonishes them as to their life on the road: "Provide yourselves with no gold or silver, not even with coppers for your purses, with no haversack for the journey or spare tunic or footwear or a staff" (Mt 10:9–10).

Immediately St. Francis knew that these were the words of assurance, the sign from God that he had been looking for, and he said, "This is what I've wanted, this is what I've been longing for with all my heart."

—St. Bonaventure, Major Life, 3:1

February 2

St. Francis Addresses Lady Poverty

Enamored of your beauty, the Son of the Most High Father clung tightly to you when he was in the world and he knew your fidelity, proven in every instance. Even before he came to earth from the splendid light of his true home, you prepared a worthy dwelling place for him, a throne to support him, a wedding bed to receive him: the Virgin most poor, from whom he was born to shine his light upon this world. And hardly was he born when you ran in haste to meet him, for he had already found his home in you instead of in easy comfort. He was laid "in a manger," the Evangelist says, "because there was no room" for him "in the living-space" (Lk 2:7). And from then on you were never separated from him and were always at his side, so that all his life long when he appeared on earth and moved among people (cf. Ba 3:38), even though "foxes have holes and the birds of the air have nests," he nevertheless had "nowhere to lay his head" (Mt 8:20). Then when he opened his mouth to teach, as in times past he had opened the mouths of the prophets, you were the first one he praised, the first one he exalted with the words "How blessed are the poor in spirit: the kingdom of heaven is theirs" (Mt 5:3).

—Sacrum Commercium, 19

February 3

The Great Almsgiver

Go humbly begging alms. Don't be ashamed, because after sin everything comes to us as an alms, and the Great Almsgiver gives generously and kindly to all, to the worthy and unworthy.

—Celano, Second Life, 77

February 4

A Royal Dignity

God is well pleased with poverty, and above all with *voluntary* poverty. For my part I possess royal dignity and special nobility, in that I follow the Lord, who was rich but became poor for our sakes (cf. 2 Co 8:9).

—Celano, Second Life, 73

February 5

Seeking and Receiving Alms

I have never been a thief of alms, seeking or using more than I needed. I always accepted less than was necessary, lest other poor people be cheated of their share.

—Mirror of Perfection, 12

February 6

The Brothers Are Not to Receive Money for Their Work

In return for the work they have done, the brothers may receive whatever they need, except money. And when the need arises, they may beg alms like other people. And they may have the instruments and tools required for their trade.

—Rule of 1221, Chapter VII

February 7

The Special Way of Salvation

Poverty is an extraordinary way of salvation, since it nourishes humility, the root of perfection. Its fruits are manifold, though hidden. This is the Gospel treasure hidden in the field. To buy it we have to sell everything, and what we cannot sell, we should consider worthless in comparison to the treasure.

—St. Bonaventure, Major Life, 7:1

February 8

The Embrace of Lady Poverty

As far as the brothers distance themselves from poverty, that far will the world distance itself from the brothers, and they will search and not find (cf. Lk 11:10). But if they remain in the embrace of my Lady Poverty, the world will nourish them, for then they are given the world for its salvation.

—Celano, Second Life, 70

February 9

The Danger of Accepting Rich Gifts

The brothers should guard against accepting churches, dwellings, even poor ones, and whatever else might be built for them, unless these are truly in keeping with the holy poverty we have promised in the Rule, and let them always dwell there only as guests, as pilgrims and strangers (cf. 1 P 2:11).

—The Testament of St. Francis

February 10

On Simple Dwellings

If at any time the brothers abandon their small, poor dwellings because someone has offered them something more spacious and comfortable, they thereby give the worst kind of scandalous example.

—Writings of Leo, Rufino, and Angelo, 61d

February 11

How to Use the New Testament

It happened once that the mother of two of the brothers came to St. Francis and his companions seeking alms. Now St. Francis used to call the mother of any of the brothers his mother and the mother of all the brothers. But when this poor woman came seeking alms, St. Francis was sad because they had nothing in the house but the New Testament which they used for prayer. So he said to his vicar, Brother Peter: "Give our mother the New Testament. And let her sell it to take care of her needs. I'm sure it is more pleasing to God that we give away the New Testament we use for prayer than hold on to it. After all, it is this very book that teaches us to help the poor."

—Celano, Second Life, 91

February 12

Helping Those in Need

Strip the altar of the Blessed Virgin Mary and cart off its varied furnishings if you cannot otherwise satisfy one who is in need. Believe me, it is dearer to Mary that the Gospel of her Son be kept, though it means stripping her altar, than to see her altar ornamented and her Son neglected.

—Celano, Second Life, 67

February 13

Lady Poverty as the Bride of the Canticle of Canticles

While he lived in this valley of tears, the Blessed Father Francis spurned the poor riches of this world and, longing for what is higher, panted with all his heart after Lady Poverty. And when he considered how she had been the constant companion of the Son of God, he abandoned everything of the world, wanting to bind her to himself with a chain of eternal love. He was enamored of her beauty; and in order to be intimately united to her as to a wife, so that the two of them would form one spirit, he not only abandoned his father and mother, but he distanced himself from all things. His Lady he held in a chaste embrace, and he was never, even for an hour, anything but a faithful spouse. This, he said to his sons, is the way of perfection, this the pledge and earnest of eternal riches.

—Celano, Second Life, 55

February 14

St. Valentine's Day

"Tell me, I pray you, where does she dwell, my Lady Poverty? Where does she dine, and where does she lie down at noon, for I am faint with love for her?"

—Sacrum Commercium, 9

February 15

St. Francis Praises Lady Poverty's Fidelity

You, most faithful spouse, sweetest lover, were never for one moment separated from your Lord. In fact, you clung all the more fiercely to him, the more others despised him. Of course, had you not been with him, he would not have been so despised by all.

You were with him amid the shouts and insults of the Pharisees, the reproaches of the chief priests; you were with him buffeted and spit upon and scourged. He deserved the veneration of all; he received mockery instead, and you alone comforted him. You did not abandon him, "even to accepting death, death on a cross" (Ph 2:8). And on the cross, when his body hung there naked, his arms outstretched, his hands and feet nailed to the wood, you suffered with him, and nothing appeared more glorious in him than you.

Then when he went to heaven, he left with you the seal of the kingdom of heaven so that you could seal the elect. Whoever, then, would sigh for the eternal kingdom must come to you, must ask you for it, and must enter it through you, for no one can enter into the kingdom without the imprint of your seal.

—Sacrum Commercium, 20–21

February 16

Choosing Holy Poverty

Never am I so ashamed than when I find someone more miserably poor than I, for I've chosen Holy Poverty for my lady, my delight, my spiritual and material treasure.

—Mirror of Perfection, 17

February 17

Lady Poverty Speaks

"I was once in the paradise of my God, where people walked naked; in fact, I walked in them and with them in their nakedness throughout that most splendid paradise, fearing nothing, doubting nothing, and suspecting no evil. I thought I would be with them forever, for the Most High created them just, good, and wise and placed them in that pleasant and beautiful place. I rejoiced exceedingly and played before them all the while, for *possessing nothing*, they belonged entirely to God."

—Sacrum Commercium, 25

February 18

Of Poverty and Weapons

The Bishop of Assisi once said to St. Francis, "I think your life is too hard, too rough. You don't possess anything in this world."

And Francis replied: "My Lord, if we had possessions, we would need weapons to defend them."

—Anonymous of Perugia, 17

February 19

St. Francis Corrects a Brother

One day St. Francis heard a brother insinuate to a poor little man who was begging an alms, "How do I know you're not really rich and pretending to be in need?"

When Francis, the Father of the Poor, heard this, he was deeply saddened. He severely rebuked the brother who had dared to utter such words and ordered him to strip before the beggar and beg his pardon, kissing his feet.

—Celano, First Life, 76

February 20

How to Endure the Winter Cold

Someone once asked St. Francis how he protected himself from the piercing cold of winter when his clothing was so poor, and he answered fervently, "If our hearts are on fire with longing for our heavenly home, we will have no trouble enduring this outer cold."

—St. Bonaventure, Major Life, 5:2

February 21

A Lazy Brother Is Chastised

In the beginning, when the Order was new and the brothers were living at Rivotorto, there was a brother who didn't pray much, who did no work, and who wouldn't go begging because he was ashamed to. But he did eat, and quite well.

Now when St. Francis was thinking over what to do about him, he received the word, through the Holy Spirit, that this brother was intent upon things of the flesh. So St. Francis said to him:

"Good-bye, Brother Fly. All you want is to eat what your brothers work for and to idle away your time instead of working in God. You're like Brother Drone, refusing to work or to produce, but eating what the good bees work for, what they produce." So that brother left, and flesh-minded man that he was, he didn't even ask forgiveness.

—Legend of Perugia, 62

February 22

The Royal Dignity of Begging

Even when St. Francis would know that his host had prepared more than enough food, he would go begging at mealtime to give the brothers an example and to honor the nobility and dignity of Lady Poverty.

He'd usually say something like this to his host: "I'm going out to beg for alms because I don't want to renounce my royal dignity, my inheritance, my vocation, and the vows the Lesser Brothers and I have made. I may come back with only a few scraps, but I shall have done what was mine to do."

—Writings of Leo, Rufino, and Angelo, 2b

February 23

St. Francis's Teaching Regarding Hypocrisy

It was winter, and he was wearing only a single habit over his holy body, and it was patched all over with coarse pieces of cloth. His guardian, who was also his companion, came by a fox hide and gave it to him, saying, "Father, you're suffering spleen and stomach pain, so I beg you, for the love of God, to let this hide be sewn on the inside of your habit. Or if that is too much to expect, at least take a small part of the hide to cover your stomach." But Francis answered: "If you want me to wear this fox skin beneath my habit, then let me wear one of equal size on the outside. Sewn there, it will show others that there is another one hidden inside, too."

—Celano, Second Life, 130

February 24

Poor and Simple Clothing

All the Lesser Brothers are to wear poor clothes and, with God's blessing, let them mend them with pieces of sackcloth or some other material. I admonish and encourage them not to look down upon or judge ill of those people they see wearing soft and colorful clothes and enjoying the choicest food and drink. Instead, let each brother criticize and judge himself.

—Rule of 1223, Chapter II

February 25

St. Francis and the Rich Young Man

Once when St. Francis was passing through the district of Borgo San Sepolcro, he came upon a village named Monte Casale. And there a young man, noble and delicate, came up to him and said, "Father, I want so much to join your brotherhood."

St. Francis answered, "Little son, you are so young and a delicate nobleman; I doubt that you could endure the harshness of our poverty."

But the young man said, "Father, are you not men like me? What you can endure, then, so can I with the grace of Christ."

This answer pleased St. Francis so much that he blessed the young man and received him into the order then and there, giving him the name Brother Angelo.

—Little Flowers of St. Francis, Chapter 26

February 26

Holding Nothing Back

Blessed are you who keep nothing back for yourself, but render "Caesar what belongs to Caesar—and God what belongs to God" (Mt 22:21).

—Admonition 11

February 27

The Sin of Appropriation

When we think of possessions, we usually have material things in mind, but St. Francis used to remind his brothers that possessions are material *and* spiritual, anything we appropriate to ourselves. For him it is not possessions which are sinful, but possessiveness, appropriating to ourselves what is not ours. He says:

"You eat from the Tree of the Knowledge of Good when you appropriate to yourself your own will, thus crediting yourself with the good which the Lord says and does in you."

—Admonition 2

February 28

A Heavenly Inheritance

The Son of God was more noble than we; nevertheless, for us he made himself poor in this world. For love of him we have chosen the way of poverty; we shouldn't, then, feel humiliated to go seeking alms. It is not seemly for the heirs of the kingdom to feel ashamed of the pledge of their heavenly inheritance.

—Celano, Second Life, 74

February 29

The True Value of Money

We must not think that the utility and value of coin or money is greater than that of stones. The devil wants to blind those who do desire and value it more. And so let us who have left all things beware, lest for so little we lose the kingdom of heaven.

—Rule of 1221, Chapter VIII

March

Lent and Easter

March 1

The Wounds of the Savior

With joy-filled devotion Francis dwelt in the heavenly mansions and in complete self-emptying he remained for long periods hidden, as it were, in the wounds of the Savior. He therefore sought out solitary places where he could cast his soul entirely upon God.

—Celano, First Life, 71

March 2

Prayer of St. Francis Before the Crucifix

Most High, Glorious God,
enlighten the darkness of my heart,
and give me correct faith,
sure hope and perfect charity,
with understanding and knowledge, Lord,
so that I may fulfill your holy and true command,
Amen.

—Writing of St. Francis

March 3

Exhortation on the Fragrant Words of Jesus

I, Brother Francis, the lesser one among you and your servant:
With the desire to kiss your feet, I pray and beseech you, in the
charity which God is, that you receive with humility and with
the love they deserve the fragrant words of our Lord Jesus
Christ, and use them well and observe them perfectly . . .

And all those men and women who receive them with goodness and ponder them and send copies to others, and then
persevere in them to the end, may the Father and the Son and
the Holy Spirit bless them. Amen.

—Letter to All the Faithful, Second Version

March 4

St. Francis and Sacred Scripture

It is good to read the testimony of the Scriptures, and it is good
to seek out the Lord our God in them. But as for me, I have
already made so much of Sacred Scripture my own that I have
more than enough for my meditation and reflection. I have
need of nothing more. I know Christ, the poor crucified one.

—Celano, Second Life, 105

March 5

What God Has Done for Us

When he was asked why he went about the countryside weeping, St. Francis said, "I should travel through all the world and, without any false shame, cry and moan over the passion of my Lord!"

—Legend of Perugia, 37

March 6

Where We Are to Gaze

Look long at the Good Shepherd, Who, to save His sheep, endured the suffering of the cross.

—Admonition 6

March 7

The Salvation of Souls

St. Francis used to say we should prefer nothing to the salvation of souls, and he said so for this reason: It was for souls that the only-begotten Son of God deigned to ascend the cross.

—St. Bonaventure, Major Life, 9:4

March 8

A Prayer of St. Francis

May the fiery and honey-sweet power of your love, O Lord, wean me from all things under heaven, so that I may die for love of your love, who deigned to die for love of my love.

> —Attributed to St. Francis by St. Bernardine of Siena and Ubertino da Casale

March 9

The Gift That Is Ours

O to have a Father in heaven, how glorious and holy and great that is! O to have a Spouse in heaven, how holy, beautiful, and lovable! O to have such a Brother, how holy and how beloved, how pleasing and lowly, peaceful and sweet and lovable and desirable above all things! And O to have such a Son, who laid down his life for his sheep and who prayed to the Father for us saying: "Holy Father, keep those you have given me true to your name" (Jn 17:11).

> —Letter to All the Faithful, Second Version

March 10

The Dream of Brother Pacifico

The first minister provincial of the brothers in France was Brother Pacifico. He was a companion of St. Francis, and was sent by him to establish the Order in France. One day he dreamed that he was taken up into paradise. He saw there many thrones, all occupied, and, higher than they, a more impressive throne which was unoccupied. When he asked whose throne it might be, he was told it was reserved for St. Francis. Sometime later he asked St. Francis how he saw himself and what he thought of himself. He answered: "I think that I am the greatest sinner in the world. Yes, without question, that is how I see myself." Pacifico protested: "How can you say that? What about all the thieves, fornicators, and murderers in the world?" But St. Francis insisted: "Listen. There is no man or woman in the world who would not be more pleasing to God than I am, had God bestowed on them the many great graces he's given me. And that is why I consider myself the worst of sinners."

—From a sermon of St. Bonaventure, October 4, 1262

March 11

Eastertime at Greccio

One day during Eastertide the brothers at the hermitage of Greccio prepared the table more daintily than they usually did with white linens and glassware. Coming down from his cell, St. Francis saw the table elevated above the ground and decorated extravagantly. But though the table was smiling, he was not. Unseen and little by little he retraced his steps, put on the hat of a poor man who was there, and, taking a staff in his hand, went outside. He waited outside the door until the brothers began to eat, for they were in the habit of not waiting for him when he did not come at the signal. They had just begun to eat when this truly poor man cried out at the door, "For the love of the Lord God, an alms, please, for this poor, sick pilgrim." The brothers answered, "Do come in, whoever you are, for the love of him whose name you have invoked." He immediately entered and appeared before them as they were eating. Oh, what astonishment that pilgrim then caused these comfortable citizens! They gave him the plate he asked for, and he withdrew and sat alone on the floor, placing the dish in the ashes.

"Now I am sitting as a Lesser Brother should sit," he said. And turning to the brothers, he said, "We should be moved by the example of the poverty of the Son of God more than others are. I saw a table richly prepared, and I thought, this is not the table of poor men who beg from door to door."

—Celano, Second Life, 61

March 12

Believing Even When You Are Tempted

Once, for several years, St. Francis suffered a serious temptation of the spirit that caused him great anguish. Then one day when he was praying at St. Mary of the Angels, he heard in spirit a voice: "Francis, if you have faith, even if it is as small as a mustard seed, you will say to the mountain, move, and it will move." The saint responded, "Lord, what is the mountain I would want to move?" And again he heard, "The mountain is your temptation." Then weeping, Francis said, "Let it be unto me, Lord, as you have said." And immediately the temptation was removed, and he was made free and wholly at peace within.

—Celano, Second Life, 115

March 13

The Lord's Bridal Ring

Temptation overcome is the ring by which the Lord espouses the soul of his servant to himself.

—Celano, Second Life, 118

March 14

In What Can We All Glory?

If you were so intelligent and wise that you had all knowledge and wisdom and you knew how to interpret all languages and could accurately divine heavenly things, in all this you could not glory; because even one demon knows more heavenly things and knows more about those of the earth than all people put together; though there may of course be some human being who has received from the Lord a special knowledge of the highest wisdom.

Likewise, if you were more handsome and more rich than others and also could work wonders, like driving out demons, all these things are only obstacles to you and none of them belongs to you, and in none of them can you glory. But in this we *can* glory: in our infirmities, in carrying every day the holy cross of our Lord Jesus Christ.

—Admonition 5

March 15

St. Francis Addresses His Brothers

Brother Francis, a man of little account and of weakness, your little servant, salutes you in him who has redeemed us and washed us in his precious Blood, in him whom, when you hear his name, you should adore with reverent fear, prostrate upon the ground. Jesus Christ the Lord, Son of the Most High, is his name, who is blessed forever and ever. Amen.

—Letter to the Whole Order

March 16

Those Who Are Our Friends

Jesus Christ, our Lord, whose footsteps we're to follow, called his betrayer "friend" and willingly handed himself over to his crucifiers. Our friends, then, are all those who unjustly inflict upon us tests and ordeals, shame and injury, sorrows and torments, martyrdom and death. They are the ones we should love most, for what they're really inflicting upon us is eternal life.

—Rule of 1221, Chapter XXII

March 17

False Honor

Did not the Lord's flock actually follow him in tribulation and persecution, shame and hunger, sickness and trial and all the rest, and thereby receive eternal life from the Lord? What a great shame, then, that while the saints actually followed in the footsteps of the Lord, we, today's servants of God, expect glory and honor simply because we can recite what they did.

—Admonition 6

March 18

Busyness and Worry

We need to be especially alert to the evil subtlety of Satan. His one desire is to keep people from having a mind and heart disposed to their Lord and God.

He circles, lusting to snatch away the human heart by the ruse of some gain or assistance and to stifle remembrance of the word and precepts of the Lord.

He wants to extinguish the light of the human heart, and so he moves in by means of worldly busyness and worry.

—Rule of 1221, Chapter XXII

March 19

Prisoners of the Devil

All you who do not live in penance and do not receive the Body and Blood of our Lord Jesus Christ and who are caught up in vices and sins and go the way of evil concupiscence and the evil desires of your flesh, and who do not observe those things you have promised the Lord, and who serve the world with your body, becoming slaves to the instincts of the flesh and the cares and preoccupations of this world, you are prisoners of the devil whose children you are and whose works you do. You are blind, because you do not see the true light, our Lord Jesus Christ; you do not have spiritual wisdom, because you do not possess the Son of God, who is the true Wisdom of the Father, and of you it is said that your wisdom has been swallowed up and that you are cursed for having turned away from God's commandments (cf. Ps 119:21). You see and know what you are doing, you know and still do what is evil; and so you knowingly lose your souls.

—Letter to All the Faithful, First Version

March 20

The Lukewarm Soul

When soul is tepid and little by little cools to grace, then flesh and blood leap forward to impose their needs.

—Mirror of Perfection, 15

March 21

The Fasting St. Francis Required of His Brothers

The brothers are to fast from the feast of All Saints to the Nativity of the Lord. Then, as to the other fast which begins with the Epiphany and lasts uninterruptedly for forty days and which the Lord sanctified with His own fast, those who keep it voluntarily, may they be blessed by the Lord, and those who do not wish to keep it, are not bound to do so. But the brothers are bound to keep the other fast which ends with the feast of the Resurrection of the Lord.

They are bound to no further fasting, then, except on Fridays. And whenever necessity requires that a brother not fast, he is not bound to corporal fasting.

—Rule of 1223, Chapter III

March 22

Brother Body

In eating and drinking, in sleeping and satisfying the other necessities of the body, you should take the measure of your own physical tolerance, so that Brother Body doesn't rebel.

—Mirror of Perfection, 97

March 23

The Importance of Prudence

I exhort you to know your own constitution; for one of you might be able to get along on less food than another, and I wouldn't want you who may need more food to think you have to imitate someone who needs less. You each must know your own physical makeup and allow your body its needs, so that it has strength to serve the spirit. For just as we are bound to avoid overindulgence in food, which harms both body and soul, we must also avoid exaggerated abstinence.

—Mirror of Perfection, 27

March 24

St. Francis's Compassion for Those Who Suffer

He turned with marvelous tenderness and compassion toward anyone afflicted with physical suffering; and when he noticed deprivation or need in anyone, he saw in that person the suffering Christ himself. The love of Christ only intensified his natural bent toward compassion.

—St. Bonaventure, Major Life, 8:5

March 25

Mirrors

When you see a poor person, you are looking at a mirror of the Lord and his poor mother. So, too, in the sick you are contemplating the kind of infirmities he took upon himself for us.

—Celano, Second Life, 85

March 26

God's Seal

The Lord was pleased to endorse and confirm the teaching and Rule of St. Francis, not only by miraculous signs, but also by the marks of his own stigmata, so that no true believer could possibly question them on external or internal evidence. And in his goodness God was pleased to affix his own seal to the Rule and teaching of St. Francis, who would never have presumed to teach or write anything other than what he received from the Lord. As he himself testifies, it was God who revealed to him the entire Rule.

—From a sermon of St. Bonaventure, October 4, 1255

March 27

Jesus Christ, Our Peace and Reconciliation

Kissing your feet and with all the love I'm capable of, I beg you to render, as far as you can, all reverence and total adoration to the Most Holy Body and Blood of our Lord Jesus Christ, in whom all things in heaven and on earth are made peaceful and are reconciled to God the Almighty (cf. Col 1:20).

—Letter to the Whole Order

March 28

How the Brothers Are to Preach to the People

All my brothers, whenever they wish, may proclaim to anyone and everyone, with the blessing of God, the following or a similar exhortation and prayer of praise:

> Fear and honor, praise and bless,
> give thanks and adore
> the Lord God All-Powerful,
> Triune and One,
> Father and Son and Holy Spirit,
> Creator of all things.
> Repent! (Mt 3:2)
> Bring forth fruits worthy of repentance,
> for you know how soon we die!
> "Give, and there will be gifts for you" (Lk 6:38).
> "Forgive, and you will be forgiven" (Lk 6:37).
> And "if you do not forgive others, your Father will
> not forgive your failings either" (Mt 6:15).
> "Confess your sins to one another" (Jm 5:16).

Blessed are you who die in repentance,
for you will be in the kingdom of heaven.
Woe to those who do not die in repentance,
for you will be children of the devil
whose co-workers you are,
and you will go into fire everlasting.
Guard yourselves and abstain
from every evil and persevere
in good unto the end.

—Rule of 1221, Chapter XXII

March 29

A Prayer of Praise

All-powerful, most holy, most high and supreme God,
Holy and just Father,
Lord, King of heaven and earth,
we thank you for yourself
for through your holy will
and through your only Son
with the Holy Spirit,
You have created all things spiritual and corporal
and, having made us in your own image and likeness,
You placed us in paradise.
Then, through our own fault, we fell.

—Rule of 1221, Chapter XXIII

March 30

A Prayer of Praise

We thank you
that through your Son you created us,
and that through the holy love you had for us

you brought about his birth
as true God and true man
by the glorious, ever-virgin, most blessed, holy Mary,
and that you willed to redeem us captives
through his cross and blood and death.

—Rule of 1221, Chapter XXIII

March 31

A Prayer of Praise

We thank you
that your Son himself will come again
in the glory of his majesty
to send the wicked ones
who have not done penance and who have not known you
into the eternal fire,
and to say to all those who have known you and have
adored you and have served you in penance:
"Come, you whom my Father has blessed,
take as your heritage the kingdom
prepared for you
since the foundation of the world" (Mt 25:34).

—Rule of 1221, Chapter XXIII

April

Pilgrimage

April 1

Pilgrims and Strangers in Christ Crucified

God called St. Francis and his companions and chose them to bear the cross of Christ in their hearts and to preach it in word and action. That is why they looked like and were in fact crucified men in their comportment and in their austere life, in their deeds and actions. And that is why they wanted more to receive shame and insults for the love of Christ than the world's vain honors or respect or praise; and that is why they were saddened when they were honored. And so they went through the world as pilgrims and strangers, with Christ crucified as their only baggage.

—Little Flowers of St. Francis, Chapter 5

April 2

The Contemplative or the Active Life?

On one occasion St. Francis said to the brothers who were closest to him: "What do you think? Should I give my time to prayer or should I go about preaching? I am a poor little simple one, with no skill in speaking; I have received the gift of prayer rather than that of preaching. Besides, in prayer we acquire graces while in preaching we deal out the graces we've received. In prayer we purify the desires of our hearts and enter into union with the one, true, and supreme Good, and we grow in virtue. In preaching, on the other hand, the dust of distraction and relaxed discipline enters the soul."

—St. Bonaventure, Major Life, 12:1

April 3

Jesus, the Answer

"In prayer we talk to God and listen to him, and we walk with the angels. But in preaching, we have to descend to the human and live among others as one of them, thinking and seeing and hearing and speaking only on the human level. But, in favor of preaching, there is one argument which seems to count more than all the rest in God's eyes and it is this: the only-begotten Son of God, who is Infinite Wisdom, descended from the Father's embrace to save souls. He renewed the world by his own example, bringing the word of salvation to human beings. The price of this salvation was his precious Blood, which washes us clean, and is a fortifying drink. He kept nothing for himself, but generously gave his all for our salvation. We then are bound to act always according to the model which we see shining in him as on a high mountain. Therefore it seems more in accord with God's will that I leave the repose of contemplation and go out into the world to work."

—St. Bonaventure, Major Life, 12:1

April 4

The First Two Brothers Join St. Francis, April 16, 1208

Brother Bernard and Brother Peter, two gentlemen of Assisi, were the first to follow St. Francis. They came to him and said quite simply, "From now on we want to stay with you and do what you do. Show us then what we should do with our belongings." Francis, overjoyed that they'd come and expressed their desire, answered lovingly, "Let's go and ask the Lord's advice."

So they headed for one of the churches of the city and, entering it, fell on their knees and prayed, "Lord God, Father of Glory, we beg you in your mercy to reveal to us what we should do." Then when they'd finished praying, they said to the priest of the church who'd been standing nearby, "Father, would you open the Gospel of our Lord Jesus Christ for us?"

The priest then opened the missal for them, since they still couldn't read too well, and these were the first words they came upon, "If you wish to be perfect, go and sell your possessions and give the money to the poor, and you will have treasure in heaven" (Mt 19:21). Then turning to another page, they read, "If anyone wants to be a follower of mine, let him renounce himself and take up his cross and follow me" (Mt 16:24). And turning the pages yet another time, they read, "Take nothing for the journey; neither staff, nor haversack, nor bread, nor money; and do not have a spare tunic" (Lk 9:3).

On hearing these words, they were filled with living joy and said, "This is what we have been longing for, this is what we've been looking for!" And the Blessed Francis said, "This will be our Rule." Then, turning to the two men, he added, "Go, then, and put into practice the advice you've heard from the Lord."

—Anonymous of Perugia, 2

April 5

The Mission of the Lesser Brothers

The truth is that the Lord chose the Lesser Brothers and sent them forth for the welfare and salvation of all souls everywhere. And not only will they be received in lands of the faithful but in lands of unbelievers as well. And as long as they fulfill what they have promised the Lord, he will take care of their needs whether they be in the lands of those who do not believe or of those who do.

—Writings of Leo, Rufino, and Angelo, 73

April 6

Our Home Is in Heaven

Francis wished that everything should sing pilgrimage and exile.

—Celano, Second Life, 60

April 7

On Those Who Preach Repentance

Have no fear of being thought insignificant or unbalanced, but preach repentance with courage and simplicity. Have faith in the Lord, who has overcome the world. His Spirit speaks in you and through you, calling men and women to turn to him and observe his precepts. You will encounter some who are faithful, meek, and well disposed; they will joyfully receive you and your words. But there will be more who are skeptical, proud, and blasphemous, and who will insult you and resist your message. Prepare yourselves, therefore, to bear everything with patience and humility.

—Legend of the Three Companions, 36

April 8

Self-Deception

Those who are preoccupied only with knowing and pointing out the way of salvation to others, and neglect their own, will arrive naked and empty-handed before Christ's judgment seat. They will bring with them nothing but bundles of shame, disappointment, and bitterness. Then shall the truth of holy humility, which is our vocation, be proclaimed, exalted, and glorified. For those who were puffed up with learning prejudiced this truth by their own lives and by their empty words. They said this truth was falsehood and they cruelly persecuted, as if they were blind, those who were really walking in the truth of holy humility.

—Mirror of Perfection, 72

April 9

We Are Like Paintings

In a panel painting representing the Lord or the Blessed Virgin, it is the Lord or Holy Virgin who is honored, while the wood and the painting claim nothing for themselves. Similarly, a servant of God is a picture of God, in which God is honored for his favor. And you may not claim credit that God is pictured through you, for compared to him you are less than the wood and the painting.

—Mirror of Perfection, 45

April 10

How the Brothers Are to Go Through the World

When the brothers go through the world, they are to carry nothing for the journey, neither sack, nor scrip, nor bread; neither money, nor staff (cf. Lk 9:3; 10:4–8).

And into whatever house they enter, let them first say, "Peace to this house!" (Lk 10:5).

—Rule of 1221, Chapter XIV

April 11

Of Those Who Injure or Take Advantage of Us

The brothers should offer no resistance to injury (cf. Mt 5:39); indeed if someone slaps them on the cheek, they should offer the other as well (cf. Mt 5:39; Lk 6:29). And if one should take their cloak, let them not hang on to their tunic.

Let them give to everyone who begs of them; and let them not seek to retrieve what someone takes away from them (cf. Lk 6:30).

—Rule of 1221, Chapter XIV

April 12

Not Being Ashamed to Beg

All the brothers should strive to follow the humility and poverty of our Lord Jesus Christ, and they should remember that it is all they are to have in the whole world; for as the Apostle says, "as long as we have food and clothing, we shall be content with that" (1 Tm 6:8). And they should rejoice when they go among those considered of little account and despicable: the poor and the weak and the sick; lepers, too, and beggars by the wayside. And when it is necessary, let the brothers beg for alms. And they are not to be ashamed; rather, they should remember that our Lord Jesus Christ, Son of the living, all-powerful God, set his face like flint (Is 50:7) and was not ashamed, though he was poor and homeless and lived on alms himself, as did the Blessed Virgin and his disciples.

—Rule of 1221, Chapter IX

April 13

Witnessing to the Gospel

You can live spiritually among nonbelievers in two ways. One way is not to enter into arguments or disputes but for the sake of the Lord to be subject to every creature (cf. 1 P 2:13) and to acknowledge that you are Christians. Another way is to proclaim God's word when you see it is pleasing to the Lord, so that those who do not believe may believe in the all-powerful God—Father and Son and Holy Spirit—Creator of everything, and in the Son who is Redeemer and Savior, and so that they

81

may be baptized as Christians; for "no one can enter the kingdom of God without being born through water and the Spirit" (Jn 3:5).

—Rule of 1221, Chapter XVI

April 14

True Learning

You have as much learning as you put into practice, and you are as good a preacher as you do what you say.

—Writings of Leo, Rufino, and Angelo, 22

April 15

Compassion

In his Last Testament, St. Francis writes, "For I, being in sin(s), thought it bitter to look at lepers, and the Lord himself led me among them, and I worked mercy with them. And when I left their company, I realized that what had seemed bitter to me, had been turned into sweetness of soul and body."

—The Testament of St. Francis

April 16

The Brothers Are Forbidden Beasts of Burden

I enjoin all my brothers, be they clerics or laics, whether they go through the world or reside somewhere, that they have no beast of burden, either with them, or in the keeping of others, or any other way.

Nor are they permitted to ride horseback unless they are constrained by infirmity or great necessity.

—Rule of 1221, Chapter XV

April 17

How the Brothers Are to Serve

All the brothers, wherever they find themselves serving or working for others, are not to be the administrators or officials or preside over the house where they are offering service. Nor are they to accept any office which would cause scandal or bring harm to their souls. But let them be the lesser ones and subject to all who dwell in the same house.

—Rule of 1221, Chapter VII

April 18

On Work and the Spirit of Prayer

Those brothers to whom the Lord has given the grace of working are to work faithfully and with dedication. Thus they will rout idleness, the enemy of the soul, and still not extinguish the spirit of holy prayer and devotion which all other temporal things must serve.

—Rule of 1223, Chapter V

April 19

Nothing of Their Own

The brothers shall acquire nothing as their own, neither house, nor place, nor anything at all. Instead, with all trust, let them go begging alms as pilgrims and strangers in this world, serving the Lord in poverty and humility, and without shame, since the Lord made himself poor for us in this world. This is the highest summit of poverty, which has made you, my most beloved brothers, heirs and kings in the kingdom of heaven; it has made you poor in material things but exalted in virtue. Let this be your portion which crosses over into the land of the living (cf. Ps 142:5).

—Rule of 1223, Chapter VI

April 20

We Take Our Cell with Us

Wherever we are or wherever we are going, we have our cell with us. For Brother Body is the cell, and the soul is the hermit who dwells in it, meditating there and praying to God. Therefore, if the soul does not preserve quiet and solitude in its own cell, of what profit is a cell made by hands?

—Legend of Perugia, 80

April 21

The Seed and the Good Ground

Let us be most careful not to be ground by the side of the road or ground among the rocks or thorns, according to what the Lord says in the Gospel:

"The seed is the word of God" (Lk 8:11). That which "fell on the edge of the path and was trampled on" (Lk 8:5) are those "who have heard" (Lk 8:12) the word and do not understand.

Then immediately "the devil comes and carries away" what was sown in the heart, "in case they should believe and be saved" (Lk 8:12).

That which falls in rocky places are those who hear the word and immediately receive it with joy, but when some tribulation or persecution attends the cause of the word, they are left immediately scandalized (cf. Mt 13:21); these have no root in them; they are inconstant because they believe only for a while and in the hour of temptation fall away (cf. Lk 8:13). That which falls among thorns are those who hear the word, but the cares of this world and the seduction of wealth and other inordinate desires enter their souls and suffocate the word and it remains barren fruit (cf. Mk 4:19).

"As for the part in the rich soil, these are people with a noble and generous heart who have heard the word and take it to themselves and yield a harvest through their perseverance" (Lk 8:15).

—Rule of 1221, Chapter XXII

April 22

In What Should We Glory?

We shouldn't flatter ourselves and boast about doing what any sinner can do. A sinner can fast, pray, weep, mortify the flesh. But this a sinner cannot do: Remain faithful to the Lord. Therefore this is what we should glory in: Rendering glory to our Lord, serving him faithfully, and acknowledging as his whatever he gives us.

—Celano, Second Life, 134

April 23

Of the Care of the Sick Brothers

If one of the brothers falls sick, wherever he may be, the other brothers are not to leave him unless one of the brothers, or more, if necessary, are chosen to serve him as they would wish to be served themselves.

—Rule of 1221, Chapter X

April 24

True Estimation of Oneself

Blessed are you, servant of God, if you do not consider yourself any better when you are honored and extolled by others than when you are considered low and simple and despised; for what you are before God, that is what you are, and no more.

—Admonition 19

April 25

Avoiding Mere Appearances

Woe to those who are satisfied with the mere appearance of a religious life. They will grow sluggish in their sloth and will not remain steadfast amid the temptations permitted to prove the just. For only those who have overcome the test, after an interval of torment from the malice of the wicked, will receive the crown of life.

—Celano, Second Life, 157

April 26

Against Calumny and Arguing

And all the brothers are to guard against speaking falsely of anyone and are to avoid verbal disputes. Rather, let them seek to keep silent whenever God gives them the grace to do so. And they are not to argue among themselves, nor with others, but they are to strive to respond with humility, saying, "We are useless servants" (Lk 17:10).

—Rule of 1221, Chapter XI

April 27

Advice for Those Who Travel

I advise, admonish, and exhort you in the Lord Jesus Christ that when you travel through the world you do not quarrel or argue or judge others; rather, be meek, peaceful and modest, courteous and humble, speaking honorably to everyone.

—Rule of 1223, Chapter III

April 28

The Rule of Pilgrims

St. Francis used to say that the rule of pilgrims is this: to take shelter under someone else's roof, to thirst after your homeland, and to make your way in peace.

—St. Bonaventure, Major Life, 7:2

April 29

The Greeting of St. Francis

The Lord revealed to me that this is to be our greeting: "The Lord give you peace."

—The Testament of St. Francis

April 30

When the Brothers Are Not Received

If the brothers are not received in one place, let them go elsewhere to do penance with the blessing of God.

—The Testament of St. Francis

May

The Holy Ladies

May 1

St. Francis's Love for Mary

He embraced the Mother of our Lord Jesus Christ with indescribable love, because she had made the Lord of Majesty our brother and had obtained mercy for us. After Christ it was Mary in whom he placed his trust and whom he chose as advocate, both for himself and his brothers.

—St. Bonaventure, Major Life, 9:3

May 2

St. Francis's Devotion to Mary

St. Francis embraced the Mother of Jesus with an inexpressible love because she it was who made the Lord of Majesty our brother. He composed special songs of praise in her honor, he poured out prayers and offered her his affection. He made her the Advocate of the Order and placed under her wings the sons he was about to leave, that she might cherish and protect them to the end.

—Celano, Second Life, 198

May 3

Mary, Virgin Made Church

Hail, my Lady, Holy Queen, Mary, Mother of God.
You are virgin made church.
You have been chosen in heaven by the Most Holy Father.
With his Most Holy Beloved Son and the Holy Spirit he
     has
consecrated you, so that in you is all fullness of grace
and every good.

—Salutation to the Blessed Virgin Mary

May 4

To Mary and All the Holy Virtues

Hail his palace, hail his tabernacle, his house.
Hail his vesture, hail his handmaid, his mother.
And hail all you holy virtues, who through the grace and
illumination of the Holy Spirit are poured into the hearts
     of
believers, so that you might transform unfaithfulness into
faithfulness to God.

—Salutation to the Blessed Virgin Mary

94

May 5

Prayer to the Virgin Mary

> Holy Virgin Mary,
> there is no one like you
> among women.
> Daughter and handmaid
> of the Most High Supreme King
> and Father in heaven,
> mother of our Most Holy Lord Jesus Christ,
> spouse of the Holy Spirit,
> pray for us.

—Office of the Passion

May 6

Feast of the Motherhood of Mary

We are mothers of our Lord Jesus Christ when we carry him in our hearts and in our bodies, lovingly, and with a pure and sincere conscience, and give birth to him through the working of his grace in us which should shine forth as an example to others.

—Letter to All the Faithful, Second Version

May 7

Spouses and Brethren of Christ

We are his spouses when our faithful souls are wed to Jesus Christ by the Holy Spirit. We are his brothers and sisters when we do the will of his Father who is in heaven.

—Letter to All the Faithful, Second Version

May 8

The Honor Due to Mary

How right it is that we honor so highly the Virgin Mary, for she carried Jesus in her most holy womb.

—Letter to the Whole Order

May 9

St. Clare Reveals a Prophecy of Francis About the Poor Ladies

Immediately after his conversion and before St. Francis had any brothers or companions, he spent his time repairing the church of San Damiano. There he received that vision of the Lord which filled him with heavenly consolation, there he made his final decision to leave the world, and there in a transport of joy and enlightened by the Holy Spirit, he prophesied something about us which the Lord later fulfilled.

He climbed the wall of the church and cried out in French to some poor people standing around, "Come and help me build this monastery of San Damiano, because in a short time some ladies are going to live here whose holy lives will bring glory to our Heavenly Father throughout the whole Church."

—The Testament of St. Clare

May 10

St. Clare Joins Francis and His Brothers

On Palm Sunday, March 18, 1212, a young noblewoman of Assisi, Clare di Favarone, attended Mass at the cathedral of San Rufino where she received her palm from the hand of the bishop himself. That night she left home secretly and went to the chapel of St. Mary of the Angels, the Portiuncula. There St. Francis himself witnessed her vows to live the Gospel life of poverty, chastity, and obedience. From that moment till her death she was a true Bride of the Poor Christ, the most faithful daughter of St. Francis.

May 11

A Canticle for the Poor Ladies

Two years before he died St. Francis sang, in the Umbrian dialect, his great song *The Canticle of Brother Sun,* and when he finished it, he sang this Song for St. Clare and her Poor Ladies:

Listen, poor little women, called by the Lord,
gathered together from many places and provinces:
Live always in truth,
so you may die in obedience.
Do not long for the life outside,
for that of the spirit is better . . .

May 12

With great love I beg you
to use discreetly the alms
which the Lord gives you . . .

May 13

Those who are heavy with sickness
and the others who are tired because of them,
all of you: bear with it in peace.
For you will sell this fatigue for a dear sum.
and each of you will be crowned queen in heaven
with the Virgin Mary.

—Collectanea Francescana 48 (1978), 5–29

May 14

The Holy Sisters

Hail, Queen Wisdom! May the Lord preserve you,
with your sister, pure and holy Simplicity.
Holy Lady Poverty, may the Lord preserve you,
with your sister, holy Humility.

Holy Lady Charity, may the Lord preserve you, with your sister, holy Obedience.

—Salutation of the Virtues

May 15

St. Francis's Last Will for St. Clare and the Poor Ladies

NOTE: Francis always referred to Clare and the other women at San Damiano as the Poor Ladies and did not want them to be called sisters or nuns.

I, Brother Francis, little one, want to follow the life and poverty of the Most High, our Lord Jesus Christ, and of his Most Holy Mother, and to persevere in this to the end. And I pray you, my ladies, and counsel you to live always in this same most holy life and poverty. Be careful to keep far from you anyone who would in any way teach or counsel anything other than this.

—Francis's Last Will for the Poor Ladies

May 16

St. Clare Echoes St. Francis's Words to His Brothers

Each of you should confidently make known your needs to the other. For if a mother loves and nourishes her daughter in the flesh, how much more lovingly should a sister love and nourish her sister in the spirit.

—Rule of St. Clare, Chapter VIII

May 17

St. Clare's Words to Those Who Have Chosen Poverty

Since the great and good Lord, on entering the Virgin's womb, chose to look despised, needy, and poor in this world, so that people in dire poverty and deprivation and in absolute need of heavenly nourishment might become rich in him by possessing the kingdom of heaven, then you who have chosen poverty should rejoice and be glad!

—First Letter of St. Clare to Blessed Agnes of Prague, 19

May 18

St. Clare Addresses Her Sisters

For the Lord himself has not only placed us as examples and mirrors for others, but also for our own sisters whom the Lord has called to our way of life, so that they in their turn will be mirrors and examples to those living in the world.

—The Testament of St. Clare, 6

May 19

St. Clare's Rule of Fasting

The sisters are to fast at all times. But on Christmas, no matter on what day of the week it falls, they may have two meals. As for the young, the frail, and the sisters who serve outside the enclosure, the abbess may mercifully dispense them from fasting, as she sees fit. But in times of evident necessity, the sisters shall not be bound to bodily fasting.

—Rule of St. Clare, Chapter III

May 20

St. Clare and Most High Poverty

The summit of Most High Poverty has made you, my dearest sisters, heirs and queens of the kingdom of heaven. It has made you poor in material things, but rich in virtue. It is your inheritance, which gives you entry into the land of the living. Hold fast to Most High Poverty, my most beloved sisters, and never wish for anything more under heaven, for love of our Lord Jesus Christ and his Most Holy Mother.

—Rule of St. Clare, Chapter VIII

May 21

St. Clare's Image of the Mirror

Because the vision of Christ is the splendor of eternal glory, the radiance of eternal light and the mirror without stain, look upon that mirror each day, O queen and spouse of Jesus Christ, and continually study your countenance within it, so that you may clothe yourself inside and out with beautiful robes and cover yourself with the flowers and garments of all the virtues, as becomes the daughter and most chaste bride of the Most High King. Indeed, blessed poverty, holy humility, and ineffable charity are reflected in that mirror, and, with the grace of God, you can contemplate them throughout the entire mirror.

—Fourth Letter of St. Clare to
Blessed Agnes of Prague, 14–19

May 22

St. Francis Addresses the Poor Ladies of San Damiano

Since by divine inspiration you have made yourselves daughters and handmaids of the Most High King, the Father of Heaven, and have embraced the Holy Spirit as your spouse, choosing to live according to the perfection of the Holy Gospel, I resolve and promise that personally and through my brothers I will always have the same special care and solicitude for you as I have for them.

—Rule of St. Clare, Chapter VI

May 23

St. Francis and St. Clare at the River

One day it happened that Francis and Clare were walking on opposite sides of a river in flood. When Francis saw Clare, he tried to cross the river to her, but the powerful, swirling current prevented him. He was troubled because dangerous water kept him from joining this sister after his own spirit. Then suddenly Clare threw her mantle on the water and, stepping on it, walked across the river in an instant. Blessed Francis, in awe and devotion, then said, "See, Lady Clare, you are more in favor with God than I am."

—A folk story of the country people of Rocca Sant'Angelo, transcribed by Arnaldo Fortini in *Nova Vita di San Francesco*

May 24

St. Francis and St. Clare

It happened once that St. Francis and Brother Leo went to Siena together, and St. Francis was sad because the people had shown them so little courtesy. He began to think of his dear Assisi where he had left his spiritual sons and his beloved daughter in God, St. Clare. He knew how much she was suffering because of her devotion to holy poverty, and he feared that she might become ill. Weighed down by these thoughts, he felt he couldn't walk any farther when he and his companion got to the place where the road turns into the hill country. He dragged himself to a well and for a long time just stood looking down into the clear water. Then he lifted his head and said joyfully to Brother Leo:

"Brother Leo, little lamb of God, what do you think I've been looking at in the water of the well?"

"The moon that is reflected there," replied Brother Leo.

"No, Brother Leo, not Sister Moon, but, through the Lord's mercy, I've been looking at the true face of our sister, Lady Clare. Her countenance is so pure and full of holy joy that all my fears are gone. I know now that she has been given that perfect joy which God gives his dear ones by pouring upon them the treasures of holy poverty."

—From a popular Franciscan legend

May 25

When the Roses Bloom

One day when St. Clare and St. Francis were walking from Spello to Assisi, they had great unrest in their hearts. For on their way they had entered a house, where they had asked for and been given a little bread and water. While they were there, they had drawn looks of malice from the people, and were forced to endure all sorts of whispering, with jokes and veiled insinuations. So they went on their way in silence. It was the cold season of the year, and the land all around was covered with snow. Soon the horizon began to grow dark. Then Francis said: "Did you understand what the people were saying about us?"

Clare gave no answer. Her heart contracted as if pressed by pincers, and she felt close to tears. "It's time to part," Francis said finally. Then Clare fell on her knees in the middle of the road. After a while she got hold of herself, stood up, and went on with her head lowered, leaving Francis behind.

The road led through a forest. All at once she lost the

strength to leave him like this, without hope or comfort, without a word of farewell.

She waited.

"When will we see each other again?"

"In summer when the roses bloom."

Then something wonderful happened. All of a sudden it seemed to both of them as if there were countless roses all around—on the branches of the juniper bushes and on the frost-covered hedges. Recovering from her astonishment Clare rushed up, plucked a bunch of roses, and laid them in Francis's hands. From that day on St. Clare and St. Francis were never separated again.

—An old Franciscan legend

May 26

The Reason for St. Francis's Reverence for Women

Once St. Francis was giving a mother and her daughter the comfort of the word of God. All the while he spoke, he never looked at them, and so when they left, his companion said to him, "Father, that holy woman and her virgin daughter came to you with such devotion; why didn't you look at them?" But the holy father answered, "Who would not be afraid to look upon a bride of Christ? A whole sermon was preached with my eyes and face when they looked at me, but not I at them."

—Celano, Second Life, 114

May 27

St. Francis and the Three Poor Women

Once when St. Francis was on the road, three poor women suddenly appeared out of nowhere. They were so similar in stature, age, and appearance that you would think a threefold matter had become perfect in a single form. Then as St. Francis approached them, they bowed reverently and saluted him with a new name: "Welcome, Lady Poverty." Then the saint was filled with indescribable joy, because there was nothing he would rather have others call him than what these women had decided upon. And because he thought these were but three poor women, he turned to the physician who was accompanying him and said, "I ask you, for the love of God, to give me something to give these poor women." The doctor immediately took out some money, got down from his horse, and gave something to each of the women. After that St. Francis and his brothers and the physician went on their way. But then, after going only a short distance, they turned around and saw nothing of the women—the plain was completely empty. They were all stunned and realized that what had happened was a miracle, for they who'd flown away more swiftly than birds were not women.

—Celano, Second Life, 93

May 28

A Lamb for Lady Jacoba

Once when St. Francis was in Rome, he had with him a little lamb which he kept out of devotion to Christ, the Beloved Lamb. And when he was about to leave, he gave it to his friend, the noble Lady Jacoba dei Settesoli, to keep in her house. Afterward, the lamb, as if instructed by Francis in the things of the spirit, always accompanied Lady Jacoba to church and stayed there with her, and would not return until she did. In the morning, if the lady was late in rising, the lamb would nudge her and wake her with his bleats, urging her by his antics to get to church. Lady Jacoba, on her part, grew quite fond of the lamb who had been Francis's disciple and was now himself a master of devotion.

—St. Bonaventure, Major Life, 8:7

May 29

Brother Jacoba

When St. Francis died, his friend Lady Jacoba, whom he always affectionately called Brother Jacoba, was led to him. Francis's vicar placed the body of Francis in her arms and said, "Here, hold now in death him whom you loved in life!" But she, her hot tears falling upon his body, cried aloud and sighed, embracing and kissing him and brushing aside her veil so that she could see him unimpeded. She looked upon that precious vessel in which was hidden an even more precious treasure, the five pearls of the wounds of Christ. In awe she contemplated Francis's body upon which God had sculpted his own wounds into a masterpiece, the wonder of the whole world. And Lady Jacoba, filled with extraordinary joy, drew new life from looking upon her dead friend.

—Celano, Treatise on the Miracles, 39

May 30

The Pure of Heart

A devout and powerful king sent two messengers, one after another, to his queen. The first returned and related the queen's reply without saying a word about the queen; he had wisely averted his eyes and did not look upon the queen. The other also returned, and after a rather brief message, he embarked upon a long eulogy to the queen's beauty. "Indeed, sire," he concluded, "I have seen a most beautiful woman; happy is he who can enjoy her!"

But the king answered him: "Unworthy servant, you've been sliding your filthy glances over my queen! It is clear that you'd like to possess what your eyes have violated."

Then he called back the first messenger and said to him, "How did the queen seem to you?" But the messenger answered, "I don't really have a very clear picture of her, sire, except that she listened willingly and with patience."

And the king, "Did she strike you as a beautiful woman?"

"Sire," the messenger replied, "that is for you to notice. I only relate the messages I receive."

The king then concluded, "You have chaste eyes; you will be pure, even in my apartments. And it is there you will now serve and share in my own comforts. But as for this lecher, get him out of my palace, lest he defile my bridal chamber."

"Who then," St. Francis said, "would not be afraid to stare at a bride of Christ?"

—Mirror of Perfection, 86

May 31

The Mystical Vision of St. Clare

The Lady Clare said that once she had had a vision in which she seemed to be carrying a jug of hot water and a hand towel to St. Francis. And she was climbing a high stairway, but it was easy going, as if she were walking on level ground. And when she reached St. Francis, he bared the nipple of his breast and said to the Virgin Clare, "Come, take, and drink." And when she had done so, St. Francis instructed her to drink a second time. This she did, and what she drank was so sweet and delightful that she could not find words to describe it.

And when she drew away, St. Francis's nipple remained between her lips. And she took it from her mouth with her hand, and it seemed to be gold so clear and bright that she saw her own reflection in it as in a mirror.

—Process of Canonization of St. Clare,
Testimony of Sister Philippa, article 29.

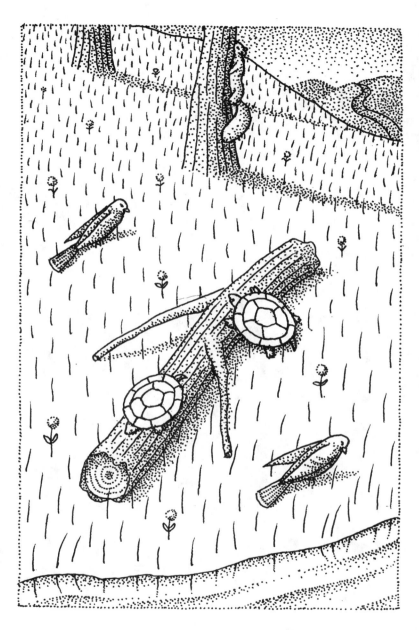

June
The Love of God

June 1

The Beginning of St. Francis's Conversion

One day, as usual, Francis was in his shop preoccupied with selling cloth when a beggar appeared asking alms for the love of God. Francis, deep in his dreams of riches, ignored him.

Then, as the beggar shuffled away, the young Francis, touched by divine grace, began to reproach himself for what he had done, thinking: "If that poor man had asked you to contribute something in the name of some count or some great baron, you'd have accommodated him, for sure. Shouldn't you have been even more eager to do so in the name of the King of Kings, the Lord of the Universe?"

And with that thought in mind, he promised himself from that moment on never to refuse a request made in the name of the Lord. Then he called the poor man back and gave him a handsome sum of money.

—Anonymous of Perugia, 4

June 2

Never Refuse Anyone Who Asks for the Love of God

One of the expressions we use in ordinary speech always moved Francis profoundly whenever he heard it, and that was, "For the love of God." As soon as he would hear these words, they would excite him, work upon him, and enkindle him, as if an inner chord had been plucked by them. And he kept faithfully till his death the promise he made to himself when he was still living a worldly life, that he would never refuse a poor person who begged anything "for the love of God." He used to say, "How greatly we should love the very love with which God has loved us so much."

—Celano, Second Life, 196

June 3

My God and My All

Lifting his eyes and hands to heaven, Francis prayed with the greatest devotion and fervor, saying, "My God and my all! My God and my all!" And he continued saying nothing but "My God and my all!" and weeping profusely until matins.

St. Francis said this prayer while contemplating in awe the excellence of the Divine Majesty which had bent down to this perishing world and was about to provide a saving remedy for Francis and others through the little poor man, Francis himself. For, enlightened by the Holy Spirit through a prophetic spirit, Francis saw the great things God was going to accomplish through him and his Order. But when he considered how inadequate he was and how meager was his virtue, he cried out in prayer to God that in his mercy, without which human frailty can do nothing, he would supply, help, and fill up what was lacking in Francis.

—Little Flowers of St. Francis, Chapter 2

June 4

The Holy Words of God

"Whoever comes from God listens to the words of God" (Jn 8:47). We who have been commissioned to deal with things divine should not only hear and fulfill what God says, but, what is more, in order to root in ourselves the transcendence of our Creator and our obedience to him, we should take reverent care of the sacred vessels and the liturgical books which contain his holy words.

—Letter to the Whole Order

June 5

Reverence for Words

I admonish you and encourage you in Christ to show all possible reverence for the written words of God wherever you may find them; and if you come upon God's words, and you see that they are not being cared for or are piled up sloppily or are scattered about, gather them up and care for them, for in honoring the words, you honor the Lord who spoke them.

How many things are sanctified by means of God's words! By the power of Christ's words, in fact, the Sacrament of the Altar is celebrated.

—Letter to the Whole Order

June 6

Reverence for the Sacrament and Word of the Lord

In this world we possess and see nothing bodily of the Most High, except his Body and Blood, and the nouns and verbs through which we were made and redeemed from death to life. Therefore, wherever the Most Holy Body has been put in an unbecoming place and left there neglected, let it be removed and placed in a secure and precious dwelling place. Likewise with the written words of the Lord that are found in unseemly places. Let us remember to gather them up and keep them in a becoming place.

—Letter to the Clergy

June 7

Holy Bread

The bread we beg is holy bread. It is made holy by our praise and love of God. When a Lesser Brother goes begging, his first words are, "Praised and blessed be the Lord our God," and then, "Give us alms for the love of the Lord our God."

—Legend of Perugia, 61

June 8

The Gifts of God

God gave and keeps on giving to each one of us a whole body, a whole soul, a whole life. He created us and redeemed us, and he will save us by his mercy alone. He has done and keeps on doing everything good for us.

—Rule of 1221, Chapter XXII

June 9

The Love of God

If St. Francis heard people use lightly the words "love of God," he didn't like it and would often rebuke them for it. He would say, "The love of God is so exalted that it should be mentioned rarely, in extreme need, and then with great reverence."

—Writings of Leo, Rufino, and Angelo, 116

June 10

What God Asks Above All Else

In holy charity, which God is, I beg all of you, that, removing every obstacle and putting aside every worry and every care as best you can, you strive to serve, love, adore, and honor the

Lord God with pure heart and pure mind, which is what he asks above all else.

—Rule of 1221, Chapter XXII

June 11

A Noble Prodigality

St. Francis used to say: "To offer the precious patrimony of the love of God in exchange for an alms is a noble prodigality, and those who value this prodigality less than money are very stupid, for only the incalculable price of divine love can purchase the kingdom of heaven."

—St. Bonaventure, Major Life, 9:1

June 12

Whenever the Bells Are Rung

You are to announce and preach to all the people his glory, so that every hour and whenever the bells are rung, all the people on earth may give praise and thanks to Almighty God.

—First Letter to the Custodes

June 13

Praises of God Most High

These are the praises which Brother Leo says Francis wrote
with his own hand on the front side of the parchment which
contains Francis's blessing to Brother Leo. The parchment is
preserved in the Convento of the Basilica of St. Francis in
Assisi.

> You are holy, Lord,
> God alone,
> who works marvels.
> You are strong.
> You are grand.
> You are Most High . . .

June 14

> You are the All-Powerful King,
> You, Holy Father,
> King of heaven and earth.
> You are three and one,
> Lord God of gods . . .

June 15

> You are the Good,
> every good,
> the highest good,
> the Lord God, living and true . . .

June 16

You are love, charity.
You are wisdom.
You are humility.
You are patience.
You are beauty.
You are safety.
You are rest.
You are joy and gladness.
You are our hope.
You are our justice.
You are temperance.
You are all our treasure overflowing . . .

June 17

You are beauty.
You are meekness.
You are our protector.
You are our guardian and defender . . .

June 18

You are strength.
You are refreshment.
You are our hope.
You are our faith.
You are our charity.
You are all our sweetness.
You are our eternal life,
great and wondrous Lord,

God All-Powerful,
merciful Savior.

—Monograph of St. Francis

June 19

To Be with Christ

Above everything else St. Francis desired "to be gone and to be with Christ" (Ph 1:23). That was why he was so concerned with freeing himself from every worldly care: lest his peace of mind be disturbed by the taint of what was mere dust. He made himself insensible to external noise and controlled his external senses and desires so that he could live absorbed in God alone.

—Celano, First Life, 71

June 20

True Love

The Lord says in the Gospel, "Love your enemies . . ." (Mt 5:44). You do in fact love your enemy when you do not brood over the evil another has done to you, but grieve instead over the sin on the other's soul, while continuing to act with love for the love of God.

—Admonition 9

June 21

St. Francis Meditates on the Our Father

"Our Father," Holiest One, our Creator, Redeemer, Comforter . . .

June 22

"Who art in heaven," in the angels and saints enlightening them to knowledge, for you, O Lord, are light; inflaming them to love, for you, O Lord, are love; dwelling in them and filling them with blessedness, for you, O Lord, are the highest good, the eternal good from whom is all good and without whom there is no good . . .

June 23

"Hallowed be thy name." May your knowledge shine in us that we may know the breadth of your benefits, the length of your promises, the height of your majesty, and the depth of your judgments . . .

June 24

"Thy kingdom come," that you may reign in us by grace and make us come to your kingdom, where there is clear vision of you, and perfect love of you, and the company and enjoyment of you . . .

June 25

"Thy will be done on earth as it is in heaven," that we may love you with our whole heart by always thinking of you; with our whole soul by always desiring you; with our whole mind by directing all our intentions to you and seeking your honor in all things; with all our strength by spending all the powers and senses of body and soul in the service of your love and not in anything else; and that we may love our neighbor even as ourselves, drawing everything, to the best of our power, to your love; rejoicing in the good of others as in our own, and being compassionate in their troubles, and giving offense to no one . . .

June 26

"Give us this day"—through remembering and understanding and reverencing the love which he had for us and for what he said, did, and suffered for us—"our daily bread," your Beloved Son, our Lord Jesus Christ . . .

June 27

"And forgive us our trespasses," by your ineffable mercy in virtue of the passion of your Beloved Son, our Lord Jesus Christ, and through the merits and intercession of the Most Blessed Virgin Mary and of all your elect . . .

June 28

"As we forgive those who trespass against us," and what we do not fully forgive, do you, O Lord, make us fully forgive, so that for your sake we may truly love our enemies and devoutly intercede for them with you, thereby rendering no evil for evil, but striving in you to do good to all . . .

June 29

"And lead us not into temptation," hidden or visible, sudden or continuous. "But deliver us from evil," past, present, and to come. Amen.

—Paraphrase of the Our Father

June 30

The Good God

All good belongs
to the Lord who is God Most High and Supreme.
Every good is his.
So let us thank him
from whom all good things come.
All honor and reverence,
all praise and blessing,
all thanks and glory
may he have and be given and receive,
he who is the Highest, the Supreme,
who alone is true God,
for every good is his
who alone is good.
And when we see or hear
someone speak or do evil
or blaspheme God,
let us speak and do what is good
and praise God,
who is blessed forever. Amen.

—Rule of 1221, Chapter XVII

July
Prayer

July 1

Prayer, a Haven of Safety

Francis's safe haven was prayer, not prayer of a few minutes, or empty, presumptuous prayer, but prolonged prayer, full of devotion and the serenity of humility. If he began late, it would be dawn before he finished. Whether walking, sitting, eating or drinking, he was rapt in prayer. At night he would retire alone to pray in abandoned, neglected churches. That was how, by God's grace, he overcame many fears and anxieties.

—Celano, First Life, 71

July 2

A Psalm for Evening Prayer

NOTE: St. Francis knew the psalms so well that he could quote many by heart or, like a great musician, he could play variations upon them, taking verses from various psalms and other scriptural passages and working them into a new whole. His own psalms, then, give us some indication of the associative workings of his mind and the breadth and depth of his knowledge of Scripture.

Clap your hands, all peoples,
acclaim God with shouts of joy.
For Yahweh, the Most High, is glorious,
the great king over all the earth (Ps 47:1–2).
Yet, God, my king from the first (Ps 74:12),
has sent his Beloved Son from on high
to bring salvation to the world.
Let the heavens rejoice and earth be glad!

129

Let the sea thunder, and all it holds!
Let the countryside exult, and all that is in it (Ps 96:11–12).
Sing a new song to Yahweh!
Sing to Yahweh, all the earth! (Ps 96:1)

—Office of the Passion

July 3

The Fragrant Words of Christ

Receive with divine love the fragrant words of our Lord Jesus
Christ. And those of you who do not know how to read should
have them read to you often, and commit them to memory,
and live them unto holiness to the end, for they are spirit and
life (cf. Jn 6:63).

—Letter to All the Faithful, First Version

July 4

Persistence in Prayer

St. Francis used to say: "If you, O servant of God, are upset, for
any reason whatever, you should immediately rise up to
prayer, and you should remain in the presence of the Most
High Father for as long as it takes for him to restore to you the
joy of your salvation."

—Celano, Second Life, 125

July 5

A Night Prayer

How long, Yahweh, will you forget me? For ever?
How long will you turn away your face from me?
How long must I nurse rebellion in my soul,
sorrow in my heart day and night?
How long is the enemy to domineer over me?
Look down, answer me, Yahweh my God!
Give light to my eyes or I shall fall into the sleep of death.

Or my foe will boast, "I have overpowered him,"
and my enemy have the joy of seeing me stumble.
As for me, I trust in your faithful love, Yahweh.
Let my heart delight in your saving help,
let me sing to Yahweh for his generosity to me,
let me sing to the name of Yahweh the Most High!

—Office of the Passion (Ps 13)

July 6

The Comfort of Prayer

Francis always sought to keep his spirit in union with God
through uninterrupted prayer, so that he would not be without
the consolations of the Beloved. In his dedication to contemplation, prayer was the comfort of his life; and as if he were
already a citizen of heaven and a fellow citizen of the angels, he
went in ardent search of the Beloved, from whom he was
separated only by a partition of flesh.

—St. Bonaventure, Major Life, 10:1

July 7

A Psalm-Prayer

Holy, Holy, Holy
is the Lord God, the Almighty;
who was, and is and is to come (Rv 4:8):
Let us praise and glorify him forever.

O Lord our God, you are worthy
to receive glory and honor and power (Rv 4:11):
Let us praise and glorify him forever.

Worthy is the Lamb that was sacrificed
to receive power, riches, wisdom,
strength, honor, glory and blessing (Rv 5:12):
Let us praise and glorify him forever.

Let us bless the Father and the Son
with the Holy Spirit:
Let us praise and glorify him forever.

Bless the Lord, all the Lord's creation (Dn 3:57):
Let us praise and glorify him forever . . .

July 8

Praise our God, you servants of his and those who
fear him, small and great alike (Rv 19:5):
Let us praise and glorify him forever.

Let heaven and earth praise him
who is glorious:
Let us praise and glorify him forever.

And all the living things in creation—
everything that lives in heaven,

and on earth, and under the earth,
and in the sea (Rv 5:13):
Let us praise and glorify him forever.

—St. Francis's Prayer Before Each Hour of the Office

July 9

The Most Holy Body and Blood of Jesus

The Father's "home is in inaccessible light" (1 Tm 6:16), and "No one has ever seen God" (Jn 1:18).

Because God is Spirit, he can be seen only in the Spirit; for "it is the spirit that gives life, the flesh has nothing to offer" (Jn 6:63).

Likewise, neither is the Son, in that he is equal to the Father, seen by anyone but the Father and the Holy Spirit. Therefore, all who saw the Lord Jesus Christ and did not believe, in the Spirit, that he was divine, the true Son of God, were condemned. And so, too, now, all who see the sacrament of the Body of Christ, which is consecrated by the words of the Lord upon the altar in the hands of the priest in the form of bread and wine, and do not see and do not believe, in the Spirit, that it is divine, indeed, the Most Holy Body and Blood of our Lord Jesus Christ, are condemned, because the Most High himself gives witness and says, "This is my body, and the blood of the covenant" (cf. Mk 14:22, 24).

—Admonition 1

July 10

Our Attitude Toward Receiving Christ in the Eucharist

Receive the Body and the Blood of our Lord Jesus Christ with great humility and with veneration, remembering the words of the Lord: "Anyone who does eat my flesh and drink my blood has eternal life" (Jn 6:54); and, "Do this in remembrance of me" (Lk 22:19).

—Rule of 1221, Chapter XX

July 11

Francis Addresses the Brothers Who Are Priests

I beseech in the Lord, all my brothers who are priests, now and in the future, and those who desire to be priests of the Most High, that when they celebrate Mass, they be pure and offer purely and with profound reverence the true sacrifice of the Most Holy Body and Blood of our Lord Jesus Christ, and that they offer it with a holy and sincere intention, and not from worldly motives or out of fear or love of some human being, as though pleasing humans (cf. Ep 6:6; Col 3:23).

But let their will, aided by the grace of God, be directed to him, desiring by means of the Mass to please the Most High God alone, because he alone works in the Mass as it pleases him.

—Letter to the Whole Order

July 12

St. Francis's Faith in Churches

The Lord gave me such faith in churches that I used to simply pray these words: "We adore you, Lord Jesus Christ, in all your churches in the whole world, and we bless you because through your holy cross you have redeemed the world."

—The Testament of St. Francis

July 13

Pray Always in Spirit and Truth

Let us adore God with pure hearts because we need to "pray continually and never lose heart" (Lk 18:1), for the Father seeks such worshipers (cf. Jn 4:23). "God is spirit, and those who worship him must worship in spirit and truth" (Jn 4:24).

—Rule of 1221, Chapter XXII

July 14

A Psalm of St. Francis

The humble have seen and are glad.
Let your courage revive, you who seek God (Ps 69:32).
Let heaven and earth and seas,
and all that stirs in them, acclaim him! (Ps 69:34)
For God will save Zion,

and rebuild the cities of Judah,
and people will live there on their own land;
the descendants of his servants will inherit it,
and those who love his name will dwell there (Ps 69:35–
36).

—Office of the Passion

July 15

The Ladder to God and Neighbor

The angelic man, Francis, like the heavenly spirits on Jacob's ladder, ascended to God and descended to his neighbor. In fact, he had learned to divide the time given him to gain merit in such a way, that he labored manfully spending part of it helping his neighbor and part in the sweet withdrawal into contemplation.

—St. Bonaventure, Major Life, 13:1

July 16

St. Francis and Solitude

The Blessed and Venerable Father Francis wanted only to be taken up with God and to purify his spirit of the dust of the world which eventually clings to us in our daily association with others. So he would periodically withdraw to a place of solitude and silence . . . He would take with him a very few companions from among those more intimately associated with his inner life, so that they might keep people from visiting or disturbing him, and might lovingly and faithfully keep guard over his quiet.

—Celano, First Life, 91

July 17

Special Graces in Prayer

When you are visited by the Lord in prayer, you should say, "Lord, you have sent me this comfort from heaven, even though I am a sinner and unworthy, and I entrust it to your keeping because I feel like a thief of your treasures." And when you leave your prayer, you should seem to be only a poor little sinner, and not someone especially graced by God.

—St. Bonaventure, Major Life, 10:4

July 18

A Psalm of St. Francis

Great is Yahweh, worthy of all praise,
more awesome than any of the gods (Ps 96:4).
Give to Yahweh, families of nations,
give to Yahweh glory and power,
give to Yahweh the glory due to his name (Ps 96:7–8)!
Offer up your selves and carry his holy cross:
follow his commandments to the end (cf. Lk 14:27).

—Office of the Passion

July 19

A Morning Prayer

I shall thank you, O Lord, Most Holy Father,
King of heaven and earth, because you have consoled me
    (cf. Is 12:1)
He is the God of my salvation:
I shall have faith and not be afraid (Is 12:2)
Yahweh is my strength and my song,
he has been my Savior (Ps 118:14).
Your right hand, Yahweh, wins glory by its strength,
your right hand, Yahweh, shatters your foes,
and by your great majesty you fell your assailants (Ex 15:6–
    7).

—Office of the Passion

July 20

How St. Francis Prayed

When Francis prayed in the wilds and in solitary places, he
would fill the woods with sighs, water the earth with tears, beat
his breast with his hand, and there, making the most of a more
intimate, secret place, he often spoke aloud with his Lord. He
would give an account to his Judge, entreat his Father, speak
with his Friend, chat amiably with his Bridegroom. Indeed, in
order to offer to God with every fiber of his being a single,
multifaceted holocaust, he would ponder the many facets of
him who is Supremely One.

—Celano, Second Life, 95

July 21

A Living Prayer

Often, without moving his lips, St. Francis would meditate for a long time and, concentrating, centering his external powers, he would rise in spirit to heaven. Thus, he directed his whole mind and affections to the one thing he was asking of God. He was not then so much a man who prayed, as a man who had become a living prayer.

—Celano, Second Life, 95

July 22

We Should Appropriate Nothing to Ourselves

St. Francis used to say things like this to his intimates: When you are at prayer and the Lord visits you with a new consolation, you should, before coming away from prayer, raise your eyes to heaven, join your hands, and say, "You have sent this sweet consolation from heaven, Lord, to me an unworthy sinner. I now give it back, so that you may keep it for me, for I feel like a thief of your treasure." And say also, "Lord, take your good gift from me in this world and keep it for me in the world to come." Thus should you speak in prayer. And when you come away from prayer, you should appear to be only a poor sinner, and not someone who has just received a new grace. For you can lose something precious for the sake of a small gratification of your vanity and easily provoke him who gave not to give again.

—Celano, Second Life, 99

July 23

Prayer to the Living God

Let us bless the Lord God,
living and true;
let us always offer him
praise and glory,
honor and blessing,
and refer every good to him.
Amen. Amen. So be it. So be it.

—Office of the Passion

July 24

The Herald of God

Every evening a herald should proclaim or use some other signal to announce to all the people that they are to render praise and thanks to the Lord God Almighty.

—Letter to the Rulers of the People

July 25

St. Francis Speaks to the Demons

Do what you want to me, wicked and deceitful spirits, for you can only do what the Lord allows you to do. Therefore I am happy to suffer everything that God lets you do to me.

—St. Bonaventure, Major Life, 10:3

July 26

Reaching Out to Others When We Are Sorely Tempted

Once when the Lord Cardinal Leo of the Holy Cross asked St. Francis to spend some time with him in Rome, the saint chose a rather secluded tower that was divided into nine arched vaults that looked like little hermit cells.

The first night, after he'd been praying to God, he was just getting ready for bed, when the demons came and began a hostile attack upon the saint of God. They assailed him so long and so vehemently that he was left as if half dead. And when they left, and he finally got his breath back, Francis called to his companion, who was sleeping under one of the other vaulted arches. And when he came, Francis said to him: "Brother, I would like for you to stay here by me, because I am afraid to be alone. Demons have just been beating me." The saint's voice was shaky and his whole body was trembling like someone in the grips of a violent fever. And so St. Francis and his companion stayed awake talking all night.

—Celano, Second Life, 119

July 27

A Prayer of St. Francis

All-powerful, most holy, most high, supreme God, all good, highest good, wholly good, who alone are good, let us give you all praise, all glory, all thanks, all honor, all blessing, and all that is good. So be it. So be it. Amen.

—Writing of St. Francis

July 28

On Praying the Divine Office

With all earnestness, I ask my lord minister general to see to it that the clerics pray the Divine Office with devotion before God, not focusing on melody of voice but on harmony of mind, so that their voices be attuned to their thoughts, and their thoughts to God. Thus they will please God by the purity of their minds, and not charm people's ears with the preciousness of their singing voices.

—Letter to the Whole Order

July 29

St. Francis's Rule for Hermitages

Those brothers who wish to live a religious life in a hermitage are to be three or at most four in number. Two of them are to act as mothers and are to have two sons or at least one. The two who perform the role of mothers are to follow the life of Martha, the other two that of Mary.

Those who follow the life of Mary are to have a cloistered space within which each one is to have his own cell in which to pray and sleep. And let them always recite compline of the day immediately after sunset. And they are to strive to preserve silence and to recite the hours, rising even for matins, and let them seek first the kingdom of God and his justice. And at the proper hour let them say prime, and after terce they may break silence, in order to speak or have recourse to their mothers; and when they wish, they may ask alms of them for the love of

142

God, just as little poor ones do. And afterward they are to say sext and none and vespers at the required times* . . .

July 30

And they are not to permit anyone to enter the cloister where they reside. And they are not to eat there. And those brothers who are the mothers must strive to keep people away and, in obedience to their minister, let them keep their sons from everyone so that no one can speak with them.

And the sons are to speak with no one, except their mothers and their minister and their custos,† when he wishes to visit them with the blessing of the Lord God.

And whenever they agree it is time to do so, the sons are to exchange roles with the mothers. And let them seek to observe all the above with most careful attention.

—The Rule for Hermitages

July 31

A Prayer for God's Will

All-powerful, eternal, just, and merciful God, grant that we poor creatures might do, by your grace, what we know you want us to do, and to want always what is pleasing to you, so that interiorly cleansed and enlightened, and inflamed by the fire of the Holy Spirit, we might follow the footsteps of your Beloved Son, our Lord Jesus Christ, and by your grace alone

* Matins, lauds, prime, terce, sext, none, vespers, and compline are the hours of the Roman Breviary, the official prayer book of the clergy.
† A minister is a local superior; a custos is a regional, provincial superior.

come to you, O Most High, you who live and reign glorified in perfect Trinity and in simple Unity, God Almighty forever and ever. Amen.

—Letter to the Whole Order

August

Joy

August 1

Putting Up with Insults and Scorn

In the beginning, when St. Francis was still wearing the clothes of a layman, although he had already renounced the world, he went about Assisi for a long time looking wretched and so emaciated by penance that many thought he'd turned simple-minded. They laughed at him as though he were mad, and relatives and strangers alike drove him away with insults and stones and mud. But he was already seasoned with a divine salt and rooted in peace of soul by the Holy Spirit, so he bore patiently all their insults and scorn with a joyful countenance, as if he were deaf and mute.

—Little Flowers of St. Francis, Chapter 2

August 2

Quiet and Meditation

Where there is quiet and meditation, there is neither preoccupation nor dissipation.

—Admonition 27

August 3

When Are We God's Servants?

I prayed that God would deign to show me when it is I am his servant and when not, for I want nothing else but to be his servant. And the Lord answered most graciously: "Know that you are truly my servant when you think, do, and say what is holy."

—Mirror of Perfection, 74

August 4

Of Blame and Praise

For his part, Francis preferred insult to praise, because he knew that insult leads to self-improvement, praise to downfall. And so when people praised his merits and holiness, he would command one of the brothers to assault his ears with phrases that humiliated and mortified him. And when the brother, although unwilling, called him uncouth and mercenary, unskilled and useless, Francis would reply, his face shining with his heart's joy, "The Lord bless you, dearest son, for you have spoken the very truth. These are the kind of words that suit well the son of Peter Bernardone."

—St. Bonaventure, Major Life, 6:1

August 5

A Warning

We must take good care that under the pretext of reward, of doing good, of giving assistance, we do not lose or turn our minds and hearts from the Lord.

—Rule of 1221, Chapter XXII

August 6

Admonition for Peacemakers

The peace which you proclaim with words must dwell even more abundantly in your hearts. Do not provoke others to anger or give scandal. Rather, let your gentleness draw them to peace, goodness, and concord. This is our vocation: to heal wounds, to bind what is broken, to bring home those who are lost. And remember that many who may now seem to be of the devil can one day become disciples of Christ.

—Legend of the Three Companions, 58

August 7

Trust in God

In his courtesy and good pleasure, God can banish the darkness and give us his wonder-working light.

—St. Bonaventure, Major Life, 5:12

August 8

The Power of Spiritual Joy

St. Francis was sure that spiritual joy is the safest remedy against the thousand snares and wiles of the enemy. He used to say, "The devil is most happy when he can snatch from a servant of God true joy of spirit. He carries dust with him to throw into the smallest chinks of conscience and thus soil one's mental candor and purity of life. But if joy of spirit fills the heart, the serpent shoots his deadly venom in vain."

—Celano, Second Life, 125

August 9

Joy Wards Off Evil

Servant of God, if you apply yourself to acquiring and preserving, both in heart and demeanor, that joy which comes from a pure heart and is won by devotion to prayer, the devils can do you no harm. They say, "This servant of God is as happy when things are going badly as when all is well, and so we cannot find an opening to enter him and hurt him."

—Mirror of Perfection, 95

August 10

Love and Wisdom

Where there is love and wisdom, there is neither fear nor ignorance.

—Admonition 27

August 11

A True Lesser Brother

I wouldn't seem to be a Lesser Brother if I didn't have the disposition I am about to describe to you. As superior of the Lesser Brothers I go to the chapter where I preach and admonish, and in the end it is said of me, "A man so unlettered and contemptible isn't fit for us. Therefore we do not want you to lead us with your lack of eloquence, your simplemindedness and ignorance." Finally I am dismissed in disgrace and scorned by all. I tell you, if I can't hear these words and keep the same expression, the same joy of soul, the same purpose of sanctity, then I am in no way a Lesser Brother.

—Celano, Second Life, 145

August 12

What Is Not True and Perfect Joy

St. Francis summoned Brother Leo and said, "Brother Leo, are you ready to take down some words?" And he answered, "I am ready."

"Write, then, this story about true joy: A messenger comes and says that all the teachers of the University of Paris have entered our Order—write that this is not true joy. Or so have all the prelates north of the Alps, and the archbishops and bishops as well, or the King of France and the King of England, too—write that neither is this true joy. Or if he announces that my brothers have gone among nonbelievers and converted them all to the faith, or that I have so much Divine Grace that I heal the sick and perform miracles—I tell you, Brother Leo, none of these things is true joy" . . .

August 13

Of True and Perfect Joy

"Father Francis, what then is true and perfect joy?"

"Well, I am returning from Perugia, say, and I arrive at our Friary of the Portiuncula very late at night. It is wintertime, muddy, and so cold that icicles have gathered at the fringes of my habit and keep cutting into my legs until they bleed. But at last, cold, and covered with mud, I make it to the entrance of the Portiuncula. I knock and knock and call out, and finally a brother comes and asks, 'Who are you?' and when I answer, 'Brother Francis,' he says, 'Go away. This isn't the hour to be wandering about. How dare you want to come in!' And when I insist, he snaps back, 'Get out of here, you simpleton, you idiot! We have brothers enough here and we don't need one more like you.' But I again move toward the door and say, 'For the love of God, please take me in tonight.' 'Absolutely not!' he says. 'Go to the Crosiers' hostel and ask them.'

"Now I tell you this: If I keep my patience through all this and do not get upset, then that is true joy and true virtue and salvation of soul."

—Dictated writing of St. Francis

August 14

On Hospitality

Anyone who comes to the brothers, friend or enemy, thief or robber, is to be received with kindness. And wherever the brothers are and anywhere they meet other brothers, they are to greet one another wholeheartedly and lovingly, and honor one another without grumbling (cf. 1 P 4:9). And they are to be careful not to look outwardly sad, like gloomy hypocrites, but they are to show themselves happy in the Lord (cf. Ph 4:4), and cheerful and truly gracious.

—Rule of 1221, Chapter VII

August 15

Joy Is Contagious

If at times temptation or despondency comes along to try me, and I see joy in my companions, then I immediately recover and let go of the temptation or depression. The joy I admire in others restores my own inward and outward joy.

—Mirror of Perfection, 96

August 16

The Innocent, Prayerful Heart

Since spiritual joy springs from the heart's innocence and the purity of incessant prayer, these are the two virtues we need to acquire and keep. Then that joy which I long to see and feel in myself and in others, that inward and outward joy, will be an edification to neighbor and a reproach to the Enemy. For sadness is his and those who follow him; rejoicing and always being happy in the Lord is ours.

—Mirror of Perfection, 95

August 17

How the Brothers Are to Conduct Themselves

Let the brothers love one another, as the Lord says, "This is my commandment: love one another, as I have loved you" (Jn 15:12).

And let them show by their deeds the love they have for one another, as the Apostle says, "Our love must be not just words or mere talk, but something active and genuine" (1 Jn 3:18).

And they are "not to go slandering other people" (Tt 3:2); nor are they to grumble or speak evil, for it is written, "Libelers and slanderers are enemies of God" (cf. Rm 1:30). And they are "to be peaceable and gentle, and always polite to people of all kinds" (Tt 3:2).

—Rule of 1221, Chapter XI

August 18

Those Who Are Happy and Blessed

All of you who love the Lord with your whole heart, with your whole soul and mind, and with all your strength (cf. Mk 12:30), and who love your neighbor as yourselves (cf. Mt 22:39), and who hate the vices and sins of the body, and receive the Body and Blood of our Lord Jesus Christ, and produce fruits worthy of penance (cf. Lk 3:8)! How happy and blessed are you who do these things and persevere in them. The Spirit of the Lord shall rest on you (cf. Is 11:2) and make his dwelling and abode in you (cf. Jn 14:23), and you are children of the Heavenly Father (cf. Mt 5:45) whose works you accomplish.

—Letter to All the Faithful, First Version

August 19

The True Witness

A theologian once asked St. Francis about this passage from Ezekiel: If you proclaim not to the wicked their wickedness, I will require their soul at your hand (Ezk 3:18). "Good Father," the theologian said, "I know many who, as far as I can tell, are in the state of mortal sin, and yet I don't point it out to them. Will then their souls be required at my hand?" But the Blessed Francis answered that he was unlettered and should be taught by the theologian rather than attempt his own interpretation of Scripture. In response the humble master said, "I've heard this passage interpreted by the learned, but I would like to hear your understanding of it." So the Blessed Francis said, "If the passage is to be applied to everyone, I would take it to mean that you should be so on fire with life and holiness that the light of your example and the manner of your speaking would be a reproach to the wicked. So, as I understand it, your life shining and your goodness spreading like a sweet odor will proclaim to the wicked their own wickedness."

—Celano, Second Life, 103

August 20

True Worshipers

Let us love God and adore him with purity of heart and mind, because he himself, singling this out above everything else, says, "True worshipers will worship the Father in spirit and truth" (Jn 4:23).

For all who adore him must adore him in spirit and truth. And let us adore him and pray to him day and night saying, "Our Father, who art in heaven," because we "need to pray continually and never lose heart" (Lk 18:1).

—Letter to All the Faithful, Second Version

August 21

A Paradox

Know that there are some things in life which are exalted and sublime before the Lord but are low and despicable in others' eyes; and other things which people consider grand and noble, in the eyes of God are counted worthless and vile.

—Second Letter to the Custodes

August 22

Guarding the Lord's Treasure

Blessed are you servants who lay up as treasure in heaven (cf. Mt 6:20) what the Lord shows you and do not desire to show it to others, hoping for personal gain from the Lord's treasure. For the same Most High will manifest your works to whomever he pleases. Blessed then are you servants who keep in your heart the secrets of the Lord (cf. Lk 2:19, 51; Lk 8:15).

—Admonition 28

August 23

Our Only Delight

Blessed are those religious who have no joy or delight except in the most holy words and works of the Lord, and who use them to lead others to the love of God in joy and gladness.

—Admonition 20

August 24

St. Francis's Love for the Angels

He was united with an unbreakable bond of love to the angelic spirits who burn with a marvelous fire and who inflame the hearts of the faithful and enable them to enter into God.

—St. Bonaventure, Major Life, 9:3

August 25

St. Francis's Letter to All the Faithful

In the name of the Lord, the Father and the Son and the Holy Spirit. Amen. To all Christians: religious, clerics, and lay people, men and women; to all who inhabit the whole world, Brother Francis, your servant and subject, offers the homage of reverence, true peace from heaven, and sincere love in the Lord. Since I am everyone's servant, I am bound to serve and to minister to everyone the fragrant words of my Lord.

—Letter to All the Faithful, Second Version

August 26

God's Minstrels

Who are God's servants but his minstrels who should comfort the human heart and lead it to spiritual joy?

—Mirror of Perfection, 100

August 27

Now That We Have Left the World

Now that we have left the world, we have nothing further to do but be solicitous in following the will of the Lord and pleasing him.

—Rule of 1221, Chapter XXII

August 28

Fear of the Lord

Where there is the fear of the Lord to guard the house, there the enemy cannot find a way to enter (cf. Lk 11:21).

—Admonition 27

August 29

Poverty and Joy

Where there is poverty and joy, there is neither cupidity nor avarice.

—Admonition 27

August 30

Patience and Humility

Where there is patience and humility, there is neither anger nor worry.

—Admonition 27

August 31

The Joy of St. Francis

When the sweetest melody of spirit would flame up in his heart, he would release it by singing in French, and the trickle of divine inspiration which his inner ear had caught would begin to overflow like a minstrel's song.

At times, as I have seen with my own eyes, he would pick up a stick from the ground and, holding it on his left arm, would draw across it another stick bent by means of a string, as if he were playing the violin. Then pretending to play, he would sing in French the praises of the Lord.

—Celano, Second Life, 127

September

Creatures

September 1

Seeing the Symbols Around Us

Francis embraced all things with an unheard of love and devotion, speaking to them of the Lord and exhorting them to praise Him. He spared lights, lamps, and candles, refusing to be responsible for extinguishing their light which he saw as a symbol of the eternal Light.

—Celano, Second Life, 165

September 2

Reverence for Stones

He walked reverently over rocks, out of consideration of him who is called Peter, the Rock. And when he came to this psalm verse, "Upon a rock you have exalted me" (cf. Ps 61:2–3), he would say, to be even more reverent, "At the feet of the Rock you have exalted me."

—Celano, Second Life, 165

September 3

The Contemplation of the Creator in Creatures

St. Francis praised the Artist in every one of his works; whatever he found in things made, he referred to their Maker. He rejoiced in all the works of the Lord's hands, and with joyful vision saw into the reason and cause that gave them life. In beautiful things he came to know Beauty itself. To him all things were good. They cried out to him, "He who made us is infinitely good." By tracing his footprints in things Francis followed the Beloved wherever he led. He made, from created things, a ladder to his throne.

—Celano, Second Life, 165

September 4

The Friend of Animals

That meekness which is so necessary, we should learn from St. Francis. For his was an extraordinary meekness, not only toward other people, but also toward animals. He called all animals "brother" or "sister" and we read in the story of his life how even wild animals came running to him as their friend and companion.

—From a sermon of St. Bonaventure,
evening, October 4, 1255

September 5

How We Fail Our Creator

Consider, O human, the wondrous dignity God has conferred upon you. He created and formed your body in the image of his Beloved Son, and your soul in his own likeness. Still, all creatures under heaven serve and know and obey their Creator in their own way better than you do.

—Admonition 5

September 6

Composing the Canticle of the Creatures

St. Francis said to his companions, "If an emperor were to give his entire kingdom to one of his servants, wouldn't that servant be filled with joy? And if, in addition, he gave him his whole empire, wouldn't the servant be even happier?" And he continued, "Then I too should rejoice in my infirmities and troubles, and take comfort in the Lord and give thanks always to God the Father, and to his only Son, our Lord Jesus Christ, and to the Holy Spirit for the great grace they've given me: namely, to know for certain, even while I am still clothed in the flesh, that I am assured of the kingdom, I an unworthy servant.

"So, for God's praise, for our consolation, and for the edification of others, I want to compose a new song, a canticle to the Lord through his creatures, whom we use every day, and without whom we cannot live and through whom the human race greatly offends its Creator. We are constantly ungrateful

for his gifts and blessings, and we do not praise the Lord,
Creator, and Giver of all good gifts, as we should."

Then he sat down and began to meditate for a while. And
afterward he began to sing, "Most High, all-powerful, good
Lord, etc.," and he taught his companions the words and the
melody.

—Mirror of Perfection, 100

September 7

The Canticle of Brother Sun

Highest, all-powerful, good Lord,
Yours is the praise, the glory, and the honor,
And every blessing.
They belong to you alone, Most High,
And no one is worthy to speak your name.

September 8

So, praised be you, my Lord, with all your creatures,
Especially Sir Brother Sun,
Who makes the day and enlightens us through you.
He is lovely and radiant and grand;
And he heralds you, his Most High Lord.

Praised be you, my Lord, through Sister Moon
And the stars.
You have hung them in heaven shining and precious and
fair.

September 9

And praise to you, my Lord, through Brother Wind,
Through air and cloud, calm, and every weather
That sustains your creatures.

Praised be you, my Lord, through Sister Water,
So very useful, humble, precious, and chaste.

September 10

Yes, and praise to you, my Lord, through Brother Fire.
Through him you illumine our night,
And he is handsome and merry, robust and strong.

September 11

Praised be you, my Lord, through our Sister Mother Earth,
Who nourishes us and teaches us,
Bringing forth all kinds of fruits and colored flowers
and herbs.

September 12

O, and praise to you, my Lord,
Through those who forgive one another in your love
And who bear sickness and trials.
Blessed are they who live on in peace,
For they will be crowned by you, Most High!

September 13

Praise to you, my Lord, through our Sister Bodily Death,
From whom no one living can escape.
How dreadful for those who die in sin,
How lovely for those who are found in your Most Holy
Will,
For the second death can do them no harm.

O praise and bless my Lord,
Thank him and serve him
Humbly but grandly!

September 14

The Praise Due to God

Because he suffered so much for us and gave us such gifts and
will continue to bestow them in time to come, let every creature that is in heaven and on earth and in the sea and in the
depths of the abyss (cf. Rv 5:13) render praise to God, and
glory and honor and blessing, because he is our virtue and our
strength: he who alone is good, who alone is Most High, alone
almighty, wondrous, glorious; who alone is holy, worthy of
praise, blessed forever and ever. Amen.

—Letter to All the Faithful, Second Version

September 15

Our Friend, Brother Fire

On one occasion the doctors agreed that a cauterization would cure St. Francis's eyes, and the brothers encouraged him to have it done. The man of God humbly agreed, realizing the operation would be helpful, though very painful, too. They therefore sent for a surgeon who came and put a searing-iron in the fire in preparation for the cauterization. But Francis, in order to calm his already trembling body, talked to the fire like a friend: "My little Brother Fire, the Most High has created you with a splendor that is the envy of all creation. He made you strong, beautiful, and useful. Be good to me now, be kind. I beg the great Lord who created you to temper your heat for me, so that you will burn gently and I may endure it." When he had finished his prayer, he traced the sign of the cross over the red-hot poker and waited unafraid. The glowing iron was then laid into his soft flesh and drawn from his ear to his eyebrow. Then Francis said of the pain the burn inflicted, "Give thanks to the Most High, for I can say truthfully that I never felt any heat or any pain." He had achieved such purity of heart that his body was in perfect harmony with his spirit, and his spirit with God. And so it happened by God's dispensation that creatures, who always serve their Maker, were made subject in a marvelous way to the will and command of Francis.

—St. Bonaventure, Major Life, 5:9

September 16

St. Francis's Devotion to the Saints

The saints and their remembrance were for Francis like a burning coal, which enkindled in him a divine fire. He venerated with most fervent devotion all the Apostles and especially Peter and Paul because of the fervor of their love for Christ.

—St. Bonaventure, Major Life, 9:3

September 17

Brothers Sun and Fire

At dawn, when the sun rises, everyone should praise God who has created Brother Sun for our service, for through him our eyes light up the day; in the evening, when night descends, everyone should praise God through Brother Fire, for through him our eyes light up the night. We are all, as it were, blind, and it is through these two brothers that the Lord gives light to our eyes. We should praise the Lord, then, in a special way for these creatures and for the others, too, who serve us day by day.

—Mirror of Perfection, 119

September 18

Brother Almond

One day Francis was filled with joy because he was beginning to enjoy God in all creatures. He went through the streets singing and inviting everyone to sing along with him. Then he came upon an almond tree, and he said, "Brother Almond, speak to me of God." And the almond tree blossomed.

—An old Franciscan legend

September 19

St. Francis Preaches to the Birds

Once near Bevagna in the Spoleto valley St. Francis saw a large flock of birds of various kinds. There were doves and crows, and those popularly called daws. Now Francis was always fervent toward creatures and showed them great tenderness, so as soon as he saw these birds, he left his companions and ran eagerly to the birds. And when he got close to them, he greeted them in his usual way. They seemed to be waiting for him; they didn't fly away as he expected them to. And so, filled with joy, he begged them to listen to the word of God. Among other things, he said this to the birds: "My Brother Birds, you should always praise your Creator and love him. He covered you with feathers and gave you wings to fly with and granted you a kingdom of pure air. He cares for you, too, without any worry on your part, though you neither sow nor reap."

At these words, as Francis and his companions later reported, the birds acknowledged his words in a wonderful fashion. They stretched out their necks and flapped their wings, and gazed at him with their beaks open. And St. Francis walked among them in fervor of spirit, brushing their heads and bodies with his tunic, and not one of them moved until he made the sign of the cross over them and gave them permission to fly away. And Francis and his companions went on their way, as well, praising and thanking God whom all creatures venerate and humbly acknowledge.

—Celano, First Life, 58; St. Bonaventure, Major Life, 12:3

September 20

Sister Lark

Sister Lark has a hood like a religious and is a humble bird who gladly goes in search of any little grain, and even if she finds something in the garbage, she picks it out and eats it. In flight she sweetly praises God like good religious who, detached from worldly things, turn ever toward heaven and who long only to praise God. The lark's garb, her plumage, is the color of the earth. Thus she offers religious an example of how not to wear elegant, flashy clothes, but moderately priced things, of the color of earth, the humblest of the elements.

—Mirror of Perfection, 113

September 21

The Little Black Hen

St. Francis had a vision of a little black hen, whose feathers and feet were those of a dove. She had so many chicks that she couldn't gather them under her wings, and so they ran all around her, beyond her reach.

When he woke up, Francis began to think about the dream, and the Holy Spirit revealed to him that the hen symbolized Francis himself. "I am that hen," he said, "because I am small in stature and black, and because I am to be simple like a dove and fly heavenward on wings of virtue. The Lord, in his mercy, has given and will give me more children, which I could never care for by myself. I need, therefore, to surrender them to Mother Church, who will protect them and gather them under the shade of her wings."

—Legend of the Three Companions, 63

September 22

Brother Pheasant

A certain nobleman from the commune of Siena sent a pheasant to the blessed Francis while the latter was sick. He accepted it with alacrity, not with the desire of eating it, but, in the way he always rejoiced over such things, out of love for the Creator. And he said to the pheasant: "May our Creator be praised, Brother Pheasant!" And to the brothers he said: "Let us see now if Brother Pheasant will stay with us, or if it will go back to its usual and more suitable haunts." One of the brothers took it, at the command of the saint, and placed it at a distance in the vineyard. Immediately, however, it came directly back to the saint's cell. Again Francis ordered it placed even farther away; but it came back with the greatest speed to the door of his cell and entered almost by force under the habits of the brothers who were standing at the door. The saint then ordered it to be fed diligently, embracing it and caressing it with soft words.

—Celano, Second Life, 170

September 23

Sister Cicada

One day when St. Francis came out of his cell, he saw a cicada on a branch of the fig tree that grew beside the door. The cicada was so close he could have reached out and touched it, but instead he stretched out his hand and said, "Come to me, little Sister Cicada." And immediately it jumped down upon his finger. St. Francis then began stroking the cicada with a finger of his other hand and inviting it to "Sing, little Sister Cicada." And as soon as the cicada heard his words, it began to sing, consoling Francis and moving him to praise God. He held the cicada in his hand for a good hour and then put it back on the branch of the fig tree where he had found it.

—Writings of Leo, Rufino, and Angelo, 75

September 24

The Little Sheep

Once in the Marches of Ancona St. Francis found a certain shepherd feeding a herd of she-goats and he-goats in the fields. Among the great number of these goats there was one little lamb going along and feeding humbly and quietly. When blessed Francis saw it, he stopped and, touched inwardly with sorrow of heart, then groaning deeply, he said to the brother who was with him: "Do you see this sheep that walks so meekly among the goats? I tell you that our Lord Jesus Christ walked in the same way meekly and humbly among the pharisees and chief priests. Therefore I ask you, my son, for love of him, to have pity with me on this little sheep. Let us pay the price and lead her away from among these goats."

—Celano, First Life, 77

September 25

Brother Rabbit

Once when St. Francis was staying at the town of Greccio, a little rabbit that had been caught in a trap was brought alive to him by a certain brother. When the most blessed man saw it, he was moved to pity and said: "Brother Rabbit, come to me. Why did you allow yourself to be tricked like this?" And as soon as the rabbit had been let go by the brother who held it, it fled to the saint, and without being forced by anyone, it lay quietly in his lap as the safest place possible. After he had rested there a little while, the holy father, caressing it with

motherly affection, released it so it could return free to the
woods. But when it had been placed upon the ground several
times and had returned each time to the saint's lap, he finally
commanded it to be carried by the brothers to the nearby
woods.

—Celano, First Life, 60

September 26

Brother Flowers

Francis told the brother gardener not to plant the whole garden with food, but to set aside a plot for those plants which in
their season would bloom with Brother Flowers. He said the
reason the brother gardener should plant this pretty little
flower bed with its sweetly scented herbs and flowering plants
was because it would invite all who saw it to praise God; for
every creature says, "God made me for you, oh human!"

—Writings of Leo, Rufino, and Angelo, 113

September 27

St. Francis and the Swallows

It happened once when St. Francis was preaching in Alviano
that he could not be heard because of the chattering of a flock
of swallows building their nests there. So St. Francis said to the
birds:

"My Sister Swallows, you have had your say. It is now my
turn to speak. Be quiet now and listen to the word of the
Lord."

Then to the astonishment of the people standing about, the

little birds fell silent and did not move until St. Francis finished preaching.

—Celano, First Life, 59

September 28

St. Francis and the Lambs Bound for Market

Once when St. Francis and his companion were passing through the Marches of Ancona, he met a men on his way to market carrying two little lambs over his shoulder. When Blessed Francis heard their bleating, he was filled with compassion. He went up to the lambs and touched them compassionately like a mother over her weeping child. Then he said to the man, "Why are you torturing my brother lambs, binding their feet this way and hanging them over your shoulder?"

"I am taking them to market to sell them because I need the money."

"And what will happen to them there?" asked Francis.

"Why, whoever buys them will slaughter them and eat them, of course."

"God forbid! This must not happen. Here, take this mantle in exchange, and give me the lambs."

Then, since the mantle was worth more than the lambs, the man quickly made the exchange.

Now Francis had borrowed the mantle that very day, because it was very cold. And so when he was trying to determine what to do about the lambs, he consulted with his companion, and then decided to give them to the man who'd lent him the mantle. He told the man to take care of the lambs and commanded him never to sell them or harm them, but to keep them and feed them and care for them conscientiously.

—Celano, First Life, 79

September 29

St. Francis and Brother Fish

Once St. Francis was sitting in a boat near a port in the lake of Rieti. A fisherman who had just caught a large carp rowed over to the saint and kindly offered him the fish. St. Francis accepted it joyfully and gracefully, and immediately began calling it "Brother." Then he placed the fish gently in the water and began praising the name of the Lord. But all the while Francis prayed, the fish continued to play beside the boat and would not leave until St. Francis finished his prayer and gave it permission to leave.

And so it was that St. Francis's total obedience to God gave him great dignity before creatures, who in turn obeyed him.

—Celano, First Life, 61

September 30

St. Francis and the Parsley

One night during his last illness Francis had a longing to eat some parsley, so he humbly asked for some. But when they asked the cook about it, he said it was impossible. "I have picked so much parsley from the garden that what little might be left I couldn't even find in daylight, leave alone at night."

But St. Francis replied, "Don't worry, my brother, just go to the garden and bring me the first herbs you lay your hands on."

So the brother went out to the garden and picked the first plants he came upon and brought them back into the house.

180

The brothers then looked over the handful of herbs and found there some leafy and tender parsley. The saint then ate a little of it and was greatly comforted. He then said to his brothers:

"My dear brothers, obey a command immediately without waiting for it to be repeated. And don't say that it is impossible, for if you are commanded something beyond your strength, holy obedience will give you the strength you lack."

—Celano, Second Life, 51

October

Transitus

October 1

St. Francis Welcomes Sister Death

Francis spent the remaining few days before his death in praise, teaching his much-beloved companions to praise Christ with him. He also asked all creatures to praise God and, using the words he'd composed earlier, exhorted them to love God. He even exhorted death itself, terrible and hated by all, to give praise; and joyfully going to meet it, he invited death to be his lodger. "Welcome," he said, "my sister Death."

—Celano, Second Life, 217

October 2

St. Francis's Instructions for His Death

As soon as my soul has left the body, strip me naked, as I stripped myself before the world, and place me on the bare ground. Then leave me there for as long as it takes to walk a mile.

—Writings of Leo, Rufino, and Angelo, 33d

October 3

The Transitus, or Passing of St. Francis

When he was dying, St. Francis made clear to his brothers the uniqueness of each person's response to Christ. He covered the wound in his side with his right hand, as if to preserve the seal of his own unique response, and he said, "I have done what was mine to do; may Christ teach you what is yours to do."

—Celano, Second Life, 214

October 4

The Feast of St. Francis

The larks are friends of daylight and shun the shadows of twilight. But on the eve that St. Francis passed from this world to Christ, just as twilight was descending, the larks rose up to the roof of his cell and began circling it with clamor of wingbeat and song. No one knew if they were singing with joy or sadness, for their voices were filled with joyful tears and sad joy, as if they were orphaned children weeping and singing their father into heaven. The city guards who were keeping watch there were filled with wonder and they summoned others to witness the sight.

—Celano, Treatise on the Miracles, 32

October 5

The Two Small Coins of St. Francis

Christ's Poor One, Francis, possessed nothing but two small coins (cf. Mk 12:42) which he could dispose of with largesse and charity: his body and his soul. But those two mites he offered to God continually, for love of Christ; he seemed always to be immolating his body with the rigor of fasting and his soul with the flame of desire: his body, a holocaust outside in the court of the temple; his soul, incense offered in the inner temple.

—St. Bonaventure, Major Life, 9:3

October 6

In Love with Christ Crucified

Jesus in agony in the Garden of Gethsemane and Mary in agony somewhere in Jerusalem, unable to do anything, having to stand helplessly by and let her only son suffer the terrible inner struggle that no one else can suffer for us. Such was St. Francis's feeling, his compassion for Christ, his Savior. He wanted somehow to suffer with Jesus, and so, two years before he died, this prayer rose from the depths of his love for the crucified Christ: "O Lord, I beg of you two graces before I die —to experience personally and in all possible fullness the pains of your bitter passion, and to feel for you the same love that moved you to sacrifice yourself for us."

—Little Flowers of St. Francis

October 7

St. Francis Consoles the Lady Clare

The week St. Francis died, St. Clare, the first little plant of the Poor Ladies of San Damiano and the marvelous disciple of Francis in the observance of evangelical perfection, feared that she was going to die before he did, because they both were gravely ill. She wept bitterly and would not be consoled, for she thought she would not see Francis before he died, he who had been her father after God, her consolation and teacher, the one who had rooted her in God's grace.

So Clare expressed her anxiety to Francis through one of the brothers. And Francis was filled with compassion for her, since he loved Clare with a special fatherly affection. But he knew he could not quiet her fears by a personal visit to her and the other Poor Ladies, so he sent her a letter blessing her and absolving her of any infraction she may have committed against his admonitions or the commands and counsels of the Son of God.

Then, in order that she might put aside all sadness, he said to the brother whom Clare had sent to him, "Go and tell the Lady Clare to put aside all displeasure and sadness that she cannot see me now, and assure her that, before she dies, both she and her sisters will see me again, and they will be filled with consolation."

—Mirror of Perfection, 108

America, and we hope to do more. It is our chosen profession, and we devote all of our time to it.

"But you and every other person need to make a habit of remembering to be kind to others who are sick, unwanted, crippled, heartbroken, aged, or alone. So, Timothy, go back and support us with prayer and material things, but always remember the nature of poverty: It is everywhere and can be relieved by each and every person in the world. I must go now. Goodbye, Timothy."

AT MOTHER TERESA'S request, I was given a tour of the infant hospital and orphanage, located about two city blocks away. It was a highly emotional experience to observe these children — tiny, diseased, and often badly bruised — found abandoned on the streets and brought to Mother Teresa and the Missionaries of Charity.

Equally sad were the young orphans lucky to be alive, but desperate for a new home. Each time I smiled, gestured, or said "Hi!" a new little friend was made. By the time my tour was complete, there were 40 or more children following me. I began to understand....

Since my conversation with Mother Teresa, the experience has become even more meaningful to me. And it has had a profound effect on my personal direction. Because of my encounter with Mother Teresa, I have realized that in my obsession to acquire material things, I had lost sight of the fact that it was only through human kindness and love that I was able to regain my own self-worth and respect. And it was then that I finally heard the message of Christ.   **CD**

A Right Tight Night

WHERE DID THE phrase "sleep tight" originate? Unlike what many believe, it has nothing to do with pulling the blankets tight to stay warm.

In colonial times, the best mattresses were suspended in bed frames by thick ropes. Unless the ropes were made tight, sleeping comfortably was almost impossible. To assure this, a huge keylike device was used, and "sleep tight" was a reminder to make the ropes firm before climbing into bed.

Richard Baumann

Trivia Quiz

1. In the New Testament, 46 women are given names. Three of these women, according to the Gospel of Luke, discovered the empty tomb on Easter morning and told the Apostles. Who were these women?

2. Today, most Christians celebrate Easter on the Sunday after the first full moon after the spring equinox, so Easter can fall any time between March 22 and April 25. Such was not always the case. One group of Christians, dubbed the Quartodecimans, chose another way to calculate the date of Easter. Who were the Quartodecimans?

3. The pope has many titles, including Bishop of Rome, Vicar of Christ, and Successor of St. Peter, Prince of the Apostles. Can you identify at least three more titles?

4. This canonized bishop, like Thomas à Becket nearly a century later, was martyred because he confronted his king. One miracle attributed to this saint involves a resuscitation of the dead. The king had accused the bishop of appropriating land for the Church without paying for it. The bishop then appealed to the man whom he had, in fact, paid for the land but who had died shortly after the transaction. This original landowner appeared before the court in his burial robes and vindicated the bishop. This saint's feast day is April 11. Who is he? Hint: The current pope was once bishop of the same city as this saint.

(Answers on page 103)

Even If You *Are* A Rocket Scientist

THE HARDEST THING in the world to understand is the income tax.

Albert Einstein

"You see," Mother Teresa told me earnestly, "the real poverty of the earth is as common in the South Bronx of New York City as it is here. The poverty we must fight is the poverty of unwanted humanity, a spiritual poverty that develops when no one cares. This poverty will never be erased by money and medicine and materials. It can only be cured by love."

Suddenly, I realized I had come to believe that almost anything could be taken care of with money. In my own personal struggle with alcohol, I could always get a drink, but what was most unbearable were my feelings of loneliness, despair, and rejection.

Mother Teresa was right. The deep hurt of feeling unwanted was far worse than the temporary pains of withdrawal from drugs

> *"The poverty we must fight is the poverty of unwanted humanity, a spiritual poverty that develops when no one cares. This poverty will never be erased by money and medicine and materials. It can only be cured by love."*

or food. How could I have forgotten all of this? I had so desperately wanted people to want me. And, in the end, it was love from others, not money, that gave me a new lease on life.

MOTHER TERESA BROKE in. "Timothy," she said, "we do need food, clothing, and other supplies here and in other materially poor areas of the world. But while this material support is very important, it is not the beginning.

"The real beginning, Timothy, is prayer," she stated confidently. "If you want to campaign, start first by encouraging people to pray for the poor of the world. Believe! Just believe and pray! Then do something for someone else — something that goes beyond the realm of a gift and into the category of sacrifice. There is no shortage of poverty in your country. Our Sisters of Charity work also in which had lingered respectfully in my mind for many years. Though she looked through me, I noticed her deep and dark eyes were strangely warm and handsome. And though her face revealed more than age, she gave me a youthful, warm, and scolding grin.

"Why have you come to see me, Timothy?" The directness of her question surprised me.

"I want to help you, Mother Teresa," I replied, "because it is my belief that you must take advantage of the two major events that have come about almost simultaneously. Of course, I am referring to the pope's visit to the United States and your winning the Nobel Prize."

MOTHER TERESA'S EXPRESSION turned to stone. "Do you think that all of this is coincidence?" she asked. "No. All this is God's work, and I would not accept this prize for myself. It is a gift to so many and a message to all humankind."

"Mother," I exclaimed, "I know you need more money and clothes and medicine. There are those who have been willing to donate, but have never known how or where to give. We can find new sources of help for you and your work, Mother Teresa." Again, her deep, dark eyes penetrated me.

Without moving an inch, she asked, "Have you ever done this kind of thing before? Do you think you really understand what our poverty is all about?"

"Yes!" I said defensively. "I once organized people to donate a dollar a month to a young Jesuit's cause in Peru. It worked out fine, Mother."

"Your thoughts are well-meaning, Timothy," she responded subtly, "but I don't believe in material things. It is not enough for people to simply give or share what they have enough of. We all must give more; in a sense, we must give until it hurts a little. Only then does it become charity, and only then will we be rewarded. This is a message from Christ Himself."

"Yes, Mother." I was a bit confused.

"I BELIEVE THAT you really do want to help," she continued, "but like so many others who come and go from this place, you seem to be missing the most important thing. Somehow, you feel money is the basic solution.

By now, my driver, Nandu, had arrived. We immediately set out, honking and weaving through the hot, crowded streets on our way to Lower Circular Drive. As we drove, I paid little attention to the beggars risking their lives in traffic for a mere rupee a day. Already, I had begun to picture my "audience" back home asking, "How did you ever get in to see that beautiful woman?"

A YOUNG WOMAN answered the door, which was located halfway down a narrow, unpaved alley. Without a word, she escorted me to a small sitting room and motioned for me to sit on a marble bench.

Soon, a nun in full habit approached. "You are here to see Mother Teresa, I am sure," she said.

> *"It is not enough for people to simply give or share what they have enough of. We all must give more; in a sense, we must give until it hurts a little."*

"Yes, Sister."

"Well, Mother is not feeling so well this morning and has asked me to postpone any visits until tomorrow. Will it be possible for you to return in the morning?"

"Oh, Sister!" I exclaimed. "I wish I could, but this was the only chance I had to see her. I must return to the United States in the morning."

"I am quite sorry, sir," she said sincerely.

"Sister," I pleaded, handing her the note, "I realize your situation but will ask only that you read this letter before I leave here. Please allow me this much."

After reading my note, she said, "Please wait."

Five minutes later, she returned with a wink and a grin, and grabbed me by the hand. "Come," she whispered, "Mother is waiting."

THERE SHE WAS, leaning an elbow on the marble railing overlooking a small courtyard. So intense and stern was her appearance that she reminded me of my grammar school principal — a vision

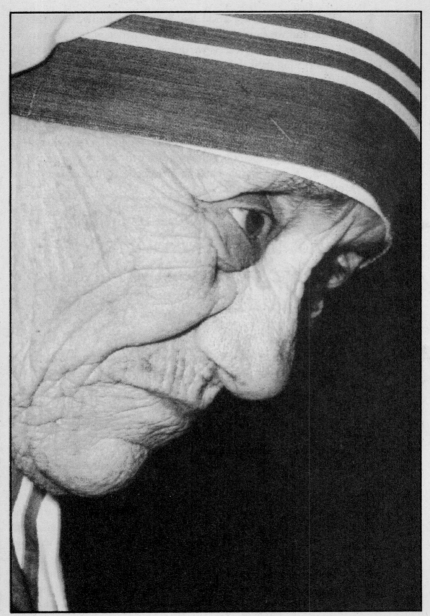

October 8

St. Francis Keeps His Promise to St. Clare

Not long after St. Clare received St. Francis's letter blessing and absolving her and the Poor Ladies, Francis died in the night. At daybreak, then, all the clergy and people of Assisi came and bore Francis's body from the place where he had died and, as they went, sang hymns of praise and waved tree branches, which they carried in his honor. And by the will of God the procession went by way of San Damiano, to fulfill the words the Lord had spoken through Francis to comfort his daughters and sisters.

The brothers removed the iron grille through which the Poor Ladies received Holy Communion and heard the Word of God, and lifted the body of Francis from its bier and placed it in the arms that reached out through the window. Lady Clare and her sisters were thereby consoled, although they were filled with grief and wept aloud that they were now deprived of the comfort and counsel of such a father.

—Mirror of Perfection, 108

October 9

St. Francis Makes a Request the Week of His Death

"You know that the Lady Jacoba of Settesoli has been, and remains, very devoted to me and to our Order. I believe that if you would let her know that I am failing, she would consider it a great favor and kindness.

"And tell her to send cloth for a tunic. It should be monk's cloth, the color of ashes, like the cloth the Cistercians weave in lands across the sea. She might also send some of that pastry she used to make for me when I was in the Holy City."

Just then there was a knock at the door. And when one of the brothers opened the outer gate, he saw before him Lady Jacoba, who explained, "Brothers, while I was in prayer I heard in the Spirit, 'Go visit your father, St. Francis, and quickly; do not delay. If you tarry, you won't find him alive. Take with you some monk's cloth for his tunic, and the ingredients you need to make that pastry for him, and take a good quantity of wax candles, too, and some incense.' "

—Writings of Leo, Rufino, and Angelo, 35a

October 10

St. Francis's Prophecy Concerning His Body

One day, when Francis lay ill in the bishop's residence in Assisi, a spiritual brother said to him with a smile, as if joking, "How much do you think you should charge the Lord for this sackcloth of yours? For much precious cloth and drapery will one day cover your little body which now is clothed in sackcloth!" And indeed, at that time St. Francis's cowl was patched with sackcloth, and his habit was all of sackcloth, as well.

Then St. Francis, or rather the Holy Spirit in him, answered with words filled with fervor and joy, "You have spoken the truth; what you've said will be fulfilled to the praise and glory of my God."

—Mirror of Perfection, 109

October 11

St. Francis's Final Psalm

It happened at the end that St. Francis was resting a few days in one of his favorite places when he realized that the time of his death was near. He therefore summoned two of his brothers and spiritual sons and commanded them to sing joyfully and in a loud voice the praises of the Lord over his approaching death, or, rather, his approaching life. Francis himself then sang, as best he could, the psalm of David which begins "Yahweh, I am calling, hurry to me, listen to my voice when I call to you" (Ps 141:1).

—Celano, First Life, 109

October 12

St. Francis Is Promised the Kingdom

One night when the many and severe pains of his sickness had exhausted him more than usual, Francis began to feel sorry for himself in the very depths of his heart. But he refused to yield to self-pity for even an hour and therefore kept praying to Christ to keep the shield of his patience unshattered. And as he continued to pray in agony, the Lord gave him the promise of eternal life in this comparison: "If the whole substance of the earth and the whole universe were priceless and precious gold, and it were given to you in exchange for these severe sufferings you are enduring, would you not be happy and willingly bear what you are suffering now?"

"Yes, I would be happy," St. Francis said. "I would rejoice beyond all measure."

"Rejoice, therefore," the Lord said to him, "your sickness is an assurance of my kingdom. Wait for it as your inheritance. Be steadfast and assured of this reward for your patience."

—Celano, Second Life, 213

October 13

God's Will

Once when Francis was very ill, he was so weak that he could not even move. But when one of the brothers asked what he would prefer to bear, this lingering, protracted illness or the suffering of an excruciating martyrdom at the hands of an executioner, he replied, "My son, what has always been and still is most dear to me and sweeter and more acceptable is whatever the Lord my God is most pleased to let happen in me and to me, for my only desire is to be found always conformed and obedient to his will in everything."

—Celano, First Life, 107

October 14

From Tears to Inner Light

St. Francis had attained a wondrous purity of soul and body, yet he never stopped purifying the eyes of his spirit with a flood of tears, despite the fact that it was damaging his bodily sight. As a result of his continual weeping, he developed a serious eye disease. But when the doctor tried to persuade him to restrain his tears if he wanted to prevent blindness, St.

Francis replied, "Brother Doctor, we shouldn't, in order to preserve that light we share in common with the flies, refuse even the smallest measure of that eternal light which visits us. The gift of sight was not given to the spirit for the good of the body, but to the body for the good of the spirit." He preferred to lose the light of his eyes rather than to dry up the fervor of his spirit by damming up his tears which cleansed his interior sight and rendered him able to see God.

—St. Bonaventure, Major Life, 5:8

October 15

The Angels Our Companions

Francis venerated most affectionately the angels who are with us on the field of battle and who walk with us in the midst of the shadow of death. We should venerate these companions, he would say, who are with us everywhere, and we should call upon them as our guardians. He used to teach that we should not offend their presence by doing in their sight what we would not do before people.

—Celano, Second Life, 197

October 16

His Last Illness

Brothers and my dearest sons, do not let my illness become a burden to you. God, in his love for me his servant, will repay you in this life and in the next, giving you the fruit of those works you cannot now attend to, because you are preoccupied with caring for me. You would not receive any greater recompense than had you done those works yourselves; for in helping me, you helped the whole Order and the very life of the brothers. You can even say to me, "We are spending a lot on your account, and the Lord will be in our debt because of you."

—Mirror of Perfection, 89

October 17

A Brief Will and Testament

St. Francis said, "Because I haven't much strength to talk, tormented as I am with the pain of my illness, I shall make three brief statements of my will concerning the brothers. In memory of the blessing and testament I leave them, they should always love and respect one another; they should always love and be faithful to our lady Holy Poverty; and they should always be loyal subjects of the prelates and priests of Holy Mother Church."

—Legend of Perugia, 62

October 18

The Final Words of St. Francis's Testament

And you who shall observe these things, may you be filled in heaven with the blessing of the Most High Father, and may you be filled on earth with the blessing of his Beloved Son together with the Most Holy Spirit the Paraclete and all the powers of heaven and all the saints. And I, Brother Francis, the littlest of the brothers, and your servant, as far as I am able, confirm for you within and without this most holy blessing.

—The Testament of St. Francis

October 19

St. Francis Blesses the City of Assisi

Lord, it is believed that in olden days this city was a refuge of evil people. But now it is clear that in your large mercy and at a time of your choosing, you have shown your special super-abundant compassion. Through your goodness alone, you have chosen Assisi to be a place of refuge for those who know you in truth, who give glory to your holy name, and who waft toward all Christian people the perfume of right reputation, holy life, true doctrine, and evangelical perfection. Therefore I pray you, O Lord Jesus Christ, father of mercies, that you not dwell on our ingratitude, but remember always the immense compassion you have shown this city. Let it always be a place of refuge for those who really know you and glorify your blessed name forever. Amen.

—Mirror of Perfection, 124

October 20

St. Francis Forgives and Blesses His Brothers

When St. Francis's death was at hand, he said to one of his brothers, "Now God is calling me. I pardon all my brothers present and absent for all their offenses and sins; and insofar as I can, I absolve them. Tell them this, and bless them for me."

—Celano, First Life, 109

October 21

The Blessing for Brother Leo

Francis wrote this blessing for his secretary and intimate companion, Brother Leo:

May the Lord bless you and keep you,
May the Lord let his face shine on you and be gracious to
  you,
May the Lord show you his face
and bring you peace (Nm 6:24–26).
The Lord bless you, Brother
                    LeTo

At the top of the piece of parchment Brother Leo himself wrote the following in red ink:

"Two years before his death, from the feast of the Assumption of the Holy Virgin Mary until the September feast of St. Michael, Brother Francis kept a Lent in the locale of La Verna in honor of the Blessed Virgin Mary, the Mother of God, and of St. Michael. After the vision and words of the seraph and the imprinting of the stigmata of Christ in his body, he made the praises written on the other side of this sheet (written in his own hand)* giving thanks for the grace bestowed on him."

Below the text of the blessing, Brother Leo wrote, again in red ink:

"With his own hand the blessed Francis wrote this blessing for me, Brother Leo."

At the bottom of the parchment there is a tau (T) with a skull and Brother Leo's note:

"Likewise with his own hand he made this sign, the tau, and the skull."

—Monograph of St. Francis

* See June 13.

October 22

The Fragrant Perfume of Holiness

St. Francis used to say that he felt filled with the sweetest fragrance (Ex 29:18) and anointed with "costly ointment" (Jn 12:3) when it was reported to him that his brothers, scattered throughout the world, were drawing many to return to the right way by the fragrant perfume of their holiness. When he heard things like this, he rejoiced in spirit and poured his enviable blessings upon those brothers who, by word and deed, were leading sinners to the love of Christ. On the other hand, those who dishonored religious life by their evil deeds incurred his condemnation and his terrible curse: "By you, Most Holy Lord, and by the whole celestial court, and by me, too, your little one, cursed be they who by their bad example disrupt and destroy what you have built up, and do not cease to build up, through the holy brothers of this Order."

—St. Bonaventure, Major Life, 8:3

October 23

The Charity of Almsgiving

Let us have charity and humility, and let us give alms, for almsgiving washes the soul of the filth of sin.

For we lose everything we leave behind in this world, but we take with us the merit of the charity and the almsgiving we've practiced and for which we will receive from the Lord a reward and worthy recompense.

—Letter to All the Faithful, Second Version

October 24

On Those Who Preach Repentance

Have no fear of being thought insignificant or unbalanced, but preach repentance with courage and simplicity. Have faith in the Lord, who has overcome the world. His Spirit speaks in you and through you, calling men and women to turn to him and observe his precepts. You will encounter some who are faithful, meek, and well disposed; they will joyfully receive you and your words. But there will be more who are skeptical, proud, and blasphemous, and who will insult you and resist your message. Prepare yourselves, therefore, to bear everything with patience and humility.

—Legend of the Three Companions, 36

October 25

Against False Security

When you are too sure of yourself, you are less on guard against the enemy. Be alert, therefore, for the devil, who, if he can claim even one hair of your head, will lose no time in making a braid of it.

—St. Bonaventure, Major Life, 5:5

October 26

St. Francis Addresses Political Leaders

Pause and reflect, for the day of death draws near. Accordingly, I beg you as respectfully as possible, do not let your cares and preoccupations with the world make you forget the Lord or turn aside from his commandments. For all those who forget him and turn away from his commands are cursed; they will be completely forgotten by him. And when the day of death does come, what you think you possess will be taken from you. And the more clever and powerful you have been in the world, so much greater will be the punishments of hell that you will have to endure.

—Letter to the Rulers of the People

October 27

A Well-Ordered Death

Once when Francis had returned from overseas, he went to preach in Celano, and a knight there invited him to dinner. So Francis and his companions went to the knight's home and were received with great joy by the whole family. Then, before they began to eat, the man of God, his eyes lifted heavenward, as was his custom, offered praise to God. But when he finished his prayer, he called his good host aside and said, "Brother Host, at your insistence I've come to eat in your home. Now at my insistence please do what I ask, because you are not going to eat here this evening, but somewhere else. Therefore, confess your sins immediately, with true contrition and repentance; and do not hide anything, but tell all with sincere sorrow. You see, the Lord is going to reward you for giving such hospitality to his little ones."

The knight then did as Francis had asked, and confessed all his sins to one of the brothers who was a priest. He put all his affairs in order and prepared to the best of his ability to meet death.

Then they all went in to dinner, and just as they began eating, the host suddenly collapsed and died, as the saint had foretold.

And so the knight merited to receive a prophet's reward because he had accorded hospitality to a prophet. That is, because of St. Francis's prophecy, the knight had repented, thereby arming himself for death and escaping eternal damnation. Instead, he was received into the eternal dwelling-places.

—St. Bonaventure, Major Life, 11:4

October 28

St. Francis's Description of the Death of the Unrepentant

You think that the vanity of this world will be yours for a long time, but you are deceiving yourself; for there will come the day and the hour that you don't think about and don't know about and ignore.

Sickness arrives, death draws near, relatives and friends come and say: Put your affairs in order. And then wife and children, relatives and friends pretend to weep. Your eyes move from face to face; and when you see their tears, you are moved by a foolish impulse and say, "Hear me! My soul, my body, everything I own, I place in your hands." Truly then are you cursed who have entrusted and exposed soul and body and all that you have into such hands. Of you the Lord says through his prophet, "Accursed be anyone who trusts in human beings" (Jr 17:5).

For immediately they summon the priest, and the priest says to you, "Do you wish to receive a penance for your sins?" And you respond, "Yes."

"Do you wish to make satisfaction, as far as you can, from your own means for your faults and for what you have gained by fraud and by deceiving others?"

And you say, "No."

And the priest says, "Why not?"

"Because I have put everything in the hands of my relatives and friends."

Then your words begin to fade out, and you die a miserable person . . .

October 29

So let everyone know, whoever you are and wherever you die in mortal sin without satisfaction, when you could have made it but did not, that the devil snatches away your soul from your body with an anguish and suffering so great that no one can know who hasn't experienced it. And all the talent and power and knowledge and wisdom that you thought you had will be taken away. And your relatives and friends take their inheritance and divide it and say, "Cursed be his soul because he could have given us more and acquired more than he did."

Then the worms begin eating your body. And thus you lose soul and body in this brief life and you go to hell where you will be tormented forever. In the name of the Father and of the Son and of the Holy Spirit. Amen.

—Letter to All the Faithful, Second Version

October 30

Words of Life

Let us cling to the words, the life, the teaching, and the Holy Gospel of him who humbled himself to petition his Father for us and make his name known to us, saying, "Father, glorify your name!" (Jn 12:28) and "glorify your Son so that your Son may glorify you" (Jn 17:1). Father, "I have revealed your name to those whom you took from the world to give me" (Jn 17:6). "I have given them the teaching you gave to me, and they have indeed accepted it and know for certain that I came from you, and have believed that it was you who sent me" (Jn 17:8).

—Rule of 1221, Chapter XXII

October 31

Let Us Begin

Though St. Francis had to moderate his early rigor because of his illness, he continued to say: "My brothers and sisters, let us begin to serve the Lord God, for up till now we have done little, or nothing."

—Celano, First Life, 103

November

The Virtues

November 1

St. Francis Exhorts His Brothers

Hear, "listen carefully to what I say" (Ac 2:14). Bend the ear of your heart and obey the voice of the Son of God. Keep his precepts in the depths of your heart and fulfill perfectly his counsels.

"Give thanks to Yahweh for he is good" (Ps 136:1) and extol him in your works, because he has sent you into the whole world for this, namely, to give testimony to his voice in word and work and to make known to all that there is no other Almighty besides him.

—Letter to the Whole Order

November 2

The Cursed and the Blessed, Happy Ones

Those who do not wish to taste how sweet the Lord is and who prefer darkness to light (cf. Jn 3:19), not wishing to observe the commandments of God, are cursed; of these the prophet says: They are "accursed, who stray from your commandments" (Ps 119:21).

On the other hand, how happy and blessed are those who love the Lord and do as the same Lord says in the Gospel, "You must love the Lord your God with all your heart, with all your soul, and with all your mind," and "your neighbor as yourself" (Mt 22:37–40).

—Letter to All the Faithful, Second Version

November 3

The True Spirit of the Lord

This is how, servant of God, you will know that you have the spirit of the Lord: If when the Lord does something good through you, the flesh does not get puffed up (for the flesh is ever in opposition to what is good); but instead, you remain less in your own eyes, less than all other people.

—Admonition 12

November 4

Rendering to God What Is His

Blessed are you, servant of God, if you attribute all that is good in yourself to the Lord God; for if you hold back anything for yourself, you hide inside yourself your Lord's money (cf. Mt 25:18), and what you think you have will be taken from you (cf. Lk 8:18).

—Admonition 18

November 5

On Not Being Angry or Troubled

No matter how someone else sins, if you let yourself be upset or angered over it, except for charity's sake, you store up for yourself—like a treasure—the sin of the other. But, servant of

God, if you do not become angry or indignant over someone else, you are living justly and poorly, that is, without claiming anything for your own.

—Admonition 11

November 6

Willingness to Bear Shame

Blessed are those servants who are not quick to excuse themselves and who humbly put up with shame and reproach for sins they are not guilty of.

—Admonition 22

November 7

On Taking Correction

Blessed are those servants who bear correction, accusation, and reproof from another as patiently as if it came from themselves.

—Admonition 20

November 8

On Patience

"Blessed are the peacemakers; they shall be recognized as children of God" (Mt 5:9).

Servant of God, you do not know how much patience and

humility you really have as long as everything goes along according to your own satisfaction. But when the time comes that instead of receiving your due, you get just the opposite, as much patience and humility as you have then is what you really have, and no more.

—Admonition 13

November 9

True Love

Blessed is that servant who would love brother or sister just as much when they are sick and cannot do anything in return, as when they are well and can.

—Admonition 24

November 10

On Having One's Faults Pointed Out

Blessed are those servants who when reproved, gently submit, respectfully obey, humbly confess and gladly make reparation.

—Admonition 22

November 11

True Humility

Blessed are you who are no more puffed up by the good which the Lord says and does through you than you are by what he says and does through others.

But sinners are you who want to receive from your neighbor more than you are willing to give of yourselves to the Lord.

—Admonition 17

November 12

Love of Neighbor

Let us love others as ourselves; and if we do not want to or cannot love them as ourselves, let us at least not do them evil, but good.

—Letter to All the Faithful, Second Version

November 13

Perfect Obedience

If you choose to suffer persecution rather than choose to be separated from your brothers and sisters, you truly stand firm in perfect obedience, for you are laying down your life for them.

—Admonition 3

November 14

Sincere Love

Blessed is the servant who would love and respect brother or sister as much when they are far away as when they are present, and would not say anything behind their back that couldn't be said with charity face to face.

—Admonition 25

November 15

Humility

St. Francis used to say: "You are what you are in God's eyes and no more."

—St. Bonaventure, Major Life, 6:1

November 16

On Peacemakers

"Blessed are the peacemakers; they shall be recognized as children of God" (Mt 5:9).

They are truly peacemakers who, in all they suffer in this world for love of our Lord Jesus Christ, preserve their peace of soul and body.

—Admonition 15

November 17

The Pure of Heart

"Blessed are the pure in heart: they shall see God" (Mt 5:8). The pure of heart are those who despise earthly things and seek those of heaven, and who never cease adoring and looking with pure heart and soul upon the Lord God living and true.

—Admonition 17

November 18

St. Francis's Reverence and Devotion to Jesus in the Eucharist

With every fiber of his being Francis burned with love for the Sacrament of the Body of the Lord. It left him overcome with wonder for so great a condescension and merciful love. He was said to be disconsolate if, even once, he could not hear daily Mass, even if it was impossible to do so. He received communion often and with such devotion as to make others experience a like devotion. He rendered every reverence to so venerable a sacrament, offering the sacrifice of his whole self; and when he received the Immolated Lamb of God, he immolated his own spirit in that fire which was always burning on the altar of his heart.

—Celano, Second Life, 201

November 19

The Grace of Prayer

St. Francis used to state firmly that we should desire the grace of prayer above everything else, and in every way possible he would encourage his brothers to the zealous practice of prayer. It was his conviction that no one could make progress in the service of God without it.

—St. Bonaventure, Major Life, 10:1

November 20

On Poverty of Spirit

"How blessed are the poor in spirit: the kingdom of heaven is theirs" (Mt 5:3). There are those who apply themselves unceasingly to prayer and to the responsibilities of office; they abstain and mortify their bodies often; but for one word that seems injurious to their person or any other thing that might detract from them, they are scandalized and thoroughly upset.

These do not have the spirit of poverty; for if you are truly poor in spirit, you hate your own life (cf. Lk 14:26) and love those who hit you on the cheek (cf. Mt 5:39).

—Admonition 14

November 21

Warning Against Hypocrisy

Beware of all pride and vainglory. Keep yourselves from the wisdom of this world and the prudence of the flesh. For the spirit of the flesh is desirous and very eager for words but does little to carry them out. And it does not seek the interior spirit of religion and holiness but desires of religion and holiness only what is outwardly apparent to people. It is of these that the Lord says, "In truth I tell you, they have had their reward" (Mt 6:2). But the Spirit of the Lord wants the flesh to be mortified and despised, worthless and rejected. And it struggles for humility and patience, and the pure and simple and true peace of the spiritual person. And above all else it is always yearning for the divine fear and wisdom and love of the Father, Son, and Holy Spirit.

—Rule of 1221, Chapter XVII

November 22

Perfect Poverty

You who long to reach the very summit of poverty must renounce not only worldly wisdom, but even, to a degree, the privilege of learning itself. Divested of these possessions, you will be able to enter in the power of Yahweh (Ps 71:16) and offer yourself naked to the embrace of the Crucified.

—St. Bonaventure, Major Life, 7:2

213

November 23

Knowledge and Good Works

The Apostle says, "The written letters kill, but the Spirit gives life" (2 Co 3:6).

They are killed by the written letter who desire to know words so that they might seem wiser than others and be able to acquire riches to leave to their relatives and friends.

And those religious are killed by the letter who do not care to follow the Spirit of Holy Scripture, but desire to know only the words and to explain them to others.

And they are brought to life by the Spirit of Holy Scripture who do not attribute to themselves everything they know and desire to know, but in word and example give credit to the Most High to whom belongs everything that is good.

—Admonition 7

November 24

The Value of Work

I want all my friars to work and to humbly occupy themselves with good works, so that we might be less of a burden to people and not stray toward laziness of heart and tongue. And whoever does not know a trade, should learn one.

—Mirror of Perfection, 75

November 25

Prudence in One's Speech

Blessed are those servants who do not talk in order to gain something and who do not reveal everything about themselves and are not quick to speak, but wisely consider what they are going to say and how they are going to answer.

—Admonition 21

November 26

Of Spiritual Murderers

There are many religious who, under the pretext of seeing better things than those which their prelates command, look back (cf. Lk 9:62) and return to the vomit of self-will (cf. Pr 26:11; 2 P 2:22). Such as these are murderers because by their bad example they cause many souls to be lost.

—Admonition 3

November 27

What Alone Is Repulsive

Nothing should be repulsive to the servant of God but sin.

—Admonition 11

November 28

On Blaming Others

There are some who, when they sin or suffer some injury, immediately blame their enemies or their neighbors. But that is not the way it is. Rather, each of us has the enemy in his or her own power, namely, the flesh by which we sin.

Therefore, "blessed that servant" (Mt 24:46) who holds captive this enemy given into his or her power and who wisely guards against it; for as long as you do this, no other enemy, visible or invisible, can do you any harm.

—Admonition 10

November 29

The Way of Holy Obedience

Holy Obedience
confounds selfish
and carnal desires,
keeps the body subject

to the obedience of the Spirit
and to obedience to one's neighbor,
rendering one submissive
to every human being
in the world;
and not only to humans,
but also to all beasts and all wild animals,
so that they can do what they want
to you insofar as the Lord
may permit them from above . . .

November 30

Holy Wisdom routs Satan
and his whole malicious band.
Pure Holy Simplicity confounds
all the wisdom of this world
and the wisdom of the flesh.
Holy Poverty confounds cupidity
and avarice and the cares of the world.
Holy Humility
confounds pride
and worldly people
and all that is of the world.
Holy Charity
routs diabolic
and carnal temptations
and all human fears.

—Salutation of the Virtues

December

Humility and the Incarnation

December 1

The Example of Christ's Humility

Humility, the guardian and ornament of all the virtues, had superabundantly filled Francis, the man of God. He thought of himself as nothing but a sinner, when in truth he was a mirror shining with all the reflections of holiness. Like the wise builder he had learned about from Christ, he wanted to build his own edifice on the foundation of humility. The Son of God, he used to say, left the womb of the Father and descended from heaven's heights into our misery to teach us by word and example, even he the Lord and Master, what humility is. Therefore he strove, as Christ's disciple, to humble himself in his own eyes and those of others, recalling what his supreme Teacher had said: "What is highly esteemed in human eyes is loathsome in the sight of God" (Lk 16:15).

—St. Bonaventure, Major Life, 6:1

December 2

The Good News of the Incarnation

Behold the Word of the Father, so worthy, so holy and glorious, whose coming the Most High Father announced from heaven in the womb of the holy and glorious Virgin Mary through his holy angel Gabriel! From the Virgin Mary's womb he received our human flesh and our frailty. "Although he was rich" (2 Co 8:9) and was placed above all things, he nevertheless decided, together with the Most Blessed Virgin Mary his mother, to choose poverty in this world.

—Letter to All the Faithful, Second Version

December 3

The Humility Befitting the Brothers

In the love which God is (1 Jn 4:16) I beseech all my brothers—speakers, workers, whether clerics or laics: Seek to humble yourselves in all things, and do not glory in yourselves or rejoice inwardly, or exalt yourselves for the good words and works or, indeed, of any good which God sometimes says or does or works in you or through you.

—Rule of 1221, Chapter XVII

December 4

The Preaching of Example

All the brothers are to preach by their works.

—Rule of 1221, Chapter XVII

December 5

Let us love the Lord God with all our hearts and
all our souls, with all our minds and all our strength
and with fortitude and with total understanding,
with all of our powers, with every effort,
every affection, every emotion,
every desire, and every wish.

—Rule of 1221, Chapter XXIII

December 6

God alone is kind
innocent
pure
from whom and through whom and in whom is
all pardon
all grace
all glory
of all the penitent and the just
of all the blessed who rejoice together in
heaven.

—Rule of 1221, Chapter XXIII

December 7

Let all of us
wherever we are
in every place
at every hour
at every time of day
everyday and continually
believe truly and humbly.

—Rule of 1221, Chapter XXIII

December 8

Let us keep God in our hearts
and love, honor, adore, serve
praise and bless
glorify and exalt him.

—Rule of 1221, Chapter XXIII

December 9

God has given and gives each one of us
our whole body, our whole soul, and our whole life.
He created us and redeemed us,
and will save us by his mercy alone . . .

—Rule of 1221, Chapter XXIII

December 10

Let us desire nothing else
let us wish for nothing else
let nothing else please us
and cause us delight
except our Creator and Redeemer and Savior,
the one true God.

—Rule of 1221, Chapter XXIII

December 11

God is the fullness of good
all good, every good, the true and supreme good.
He alone is good
merciful and gentle
delectable and sweet.
He alone is holy
just and true
holy and right.

—Rule of 1221, Chapter XXIII

December 12

Let us magnify and give thanks to
the Most High and Supreme Eternal God
Trinity and Unity
the Father and the Son and the Holy Spirit
Creator of all
Savior of all who believe in him
and hope in him
and love him.

—Rule of 1221, Chapter XXIII

December 13

God is
without beginning and without end
unchangeable, invisible,
indescribable, ineffable,
incomprehensible, unfathomable,

225

blessed, worthy of praise,
glorious, exalted on high, sublime,
most high, gentle, lovable,
delectable and totally desirable above all else
forever.
Amen.

—Rule of 1221, Chapter XXIII

December 14

St. Francis's Love for Jesus

Francis was intimately united with Jesus—Jesus always in his heart, Jesus on his lips, Jesus in his ears, Jesus in his eyes, Jesus in his hands, Jesus in all the other members of his body. How many times he would be eating dinner and would hear or mention or think about Jesus and forget to eat, so that, as we read about one of the saints, "looking he did not see, and listening he did not hear!" Often when he was on a journey, meditating or singing about Jesus, he would leave the road and start inviting all creatures to praise Jesus.

—Celano, First Life, 115

December 15

A Psalm of St. Francis

Glory to God in the highest heaven,
and on earth peace for those he favors (Lk 2:14).
Let the heavens rejoice and earth be glad!
Let the sea thunder, and all it holds!
Let the countryside exult, and all that is in it (Ps 96:11–12).
Sing a new song to Yahweh!

Sing to Yahweh, all the earth! (Ps 96:1).
Great is Yahweh, worthy of all praise,
more awesome than any of the gods (Ps 96:4).
Give to Yahweh, families of nations,
give to Yahweh glory and power,
give to Yahweh the glory due to his name! (Ps 96:7–8).
Take up your bodies and carry his cross (cf. Lk 14:27) and
follow his most holy precepts to the very end.

—Office of the Passion

December 16

St. Francis's Devotion to the Birth of Jesus

Francis used to observe with inexpressible eagerness and
above all other solemnities the Birth of the Child Jesus, calling
it the feast of feasts on which God, become a little baby, hung
upon human breasts. He would avidly kiss pictures of those
infant limbs, and his compassion for the child overflowed his
heart, making him stammer sweet words, even like a child. The
name Baby Jesus was for him honeycomb-sweet in the mouth.

—Celano, Second Life, 199

December 17

Fasting on Christmas

One Christmas the brothers were discussing whether or not
they were obliged to abstain from meat since the feast fell on a
Friday. Francis responded to Brother Morico, "You sin, little
brother, to call the day on which the Child was born for us a

Friday. On a day like this I want even the walls to eat meat, and if they can't, at least let their surfaces be smeared with it."

—Celano, Second Life, 199

December 18

A Special Law for Christmas

If I ever have the opportunity to talk with the emperor, I'll beg him, for the love of God and me, to enact a special law: No one is to capture or kill our sisters the larks or do them any harm. Furthermore, all mayors and lords of castles and towns are required each year on Christmas Day to order their subjects to scatter wheat and other grain on the roads outside the walls so that our sisters the larks and other birds might have something to eat on so festive a day. And on Christmas Eve, out of reverence for the Son of God, whom on that night the Virgin Mary placed in a manger between the ox and the ass, anyone having an ox or an ass is to feed it a generous portion of choice fodder. And on Christmas Day the rich are to give the poor the finest food in abundance.

—Mirror of Perfection, 114

December 19

A Psalm for Christmas

Sing for joy to God our strength (Ps 81:1),
acclaim the Lord God living and true with shouts of joy (cf. Ps 47:1).
For Yahweh, the Most High, is glorious,
the great king over all the earth (Ps 47:2).

228

Because the Most Holy Father of Heaven, our king from the first (cf. Ps 74:12), sent his beloved Son from on high and he was born of the blessed, holy Virgin Mary.

"He will cry to me, 'You are my father' . . . So I shall make him my first-born, the highest of earthly kings" (Ps 89:26–27). On that day the Lord bestowed his mercy and that night his song (cf. Ps 42:8).

This is the day which Yahweh has made,
a day for us to rejoice and be glad (Ps 118:24).

For the Most Holy Beloved Child was given to us and was born for us (cf. Is 9:5) on the way and was laid in a manger, because there was no room at the inn (cf. Lk 2:7).

—Office of the Passion

December 20

The First Christmas Crib

Francis's highest intention, his dominant desire, his firmest will was to observe perfectly and always the Holy Gospel, and with all vigilance, with all zeal, with all the longing of his mind and heart to follow the teaching and footsteps of our Lord Jesus Christ. He would meditate continually on Christ's words and never lose sight of his deeds. But above all, the humility of the incarnation and the charity of the passion was so imprinted upon his memory that it was difficult for him to think of anything else. So with this in mind, what he did on the birthday of our Lord Jesus Christ near the little town of Greccio in the third year before his glorious death should be devoutly celebrated and reverently remembered each year . . .

December 21

There was a certain man in Greccio by the name of John, of good reputation and an even better life. He was very dear to Blessed Francis because, although noble and greatly honored in that region, he preferred nobility of spirit to that of the flesh. Thus it was that about two weeks before the Birth of the Lord, Blessed Francis sent for this man, as he had on other occasions, and said to him, "If you would like to celebrate the Birth of Jesus at the hermitage of Greccio, then go with haste and diligently prepare what I tell you. For I wish to re-create the birth of the Babe born in Bethlehem, so that we will see with our own eyes how he did not even have the barest necessities, how he lay in a manger, how, with an ox and an ass standing by, he lay upon the hay where he had been placed." When the good and faithful man heard these things, he ran with haste and prepared the place according to Francis's instructions . . .

December 22

Now the day of joy drew near, the time of great rejoicing! For this occasion many of the brothers were summoned from various places. Men and women of the neighborhood came too, dressed in their festive native costumes, and they carried candles and torches, according to their means, to light up that night whose heavenly star lights up all our days and years. And when the Blessed Francis himself came, and found all things prepared, he was filled with joy. Then the manger itself was prepared with the hay that had been brought, and the ox and ass were led in . . .

December 23

Then was Gospel simplicity resplendent, poverty exalted, humility commended, and Greccio, as it were, a new Bethlehem. The night was bright as if full of daylight, and it was sweet to people and beasts alike. The good folk came and were filled with joy as if for the first time over a whole new mystery. The woods rang with voices, the rocks echoed their festive chorus, the brothers sang choice praises to the Lord, and the whole night seemed to leap rejoicing. The saint of God stood ecstatically before the manger, his spirit trembling with compassion and ineffable love. Then the priest celebrated the solemnity of the Eucharist over the manger and he too experienced a consolation he'd never tasted before.

—Celano, First Life, 84–85

December 24

The Little Baby of Bethlehem

Francis was clothed with the vestments of the deacon, for he was a deacon, and he sang the Holy Gospel in a resonant voice. And his voice was a strong voice and sweet, a clear voice and sonorous, ravishing everyone there with heavenly desires. Then he spoke to the people charming words about the poor King re-born and about the little town of Bethlehem. Frequently, too, when he wished to refer to Christ Jesus, he would call him simply "the Little Baby of Bethlehem," and at the word "Bethlehem" his voice was more like the bleating of a sheep. And when he said the name "Little Baby of Bethlehem" or "Jesus," his tongue licked his lips, as if he were savoring the sweetness of the words . . .

December 25

The gifts of the Almighty were multiplied at Greccio, and a wonderful vision was seen by a virtuous man who was present at the Mass. He saw the little Child lying in the manger seemingly lifeless, and then Francis, the holy man of God, went up to it and roused the Child as from a deep sleep. This vision was not unfitting, for the Child Jesus, who had been forgotten in the hearts of many, was brought to life again by God's grace working through his servant Francis and was stamped deeply upon his memory. And when the solemn vigil of Christmas was brought to a close, each one returned home with unspeakable joy.

—Celano, First Life, 86

December 26

The Miracle of the Hay

The hay that had been placed in the manger at Greccio was kept, so that the Lord might save beasts of burden and other animals through it. And in truth it happened that many animals throughout that region, beasts of burden and others with various illnesses, were freed from their ailments after eating of this hay. Indeed, even some women who had been laboring for a long time in a difficult birth delivered their children easily when some of this hay was placed upon them; and a large number of persons of both sexes, suffering from various illnesses, obtained the health they sought in the same way.

Today, the place on which the manger stood is consecrated to the Lord by a church, and over the manger there is an altar dedicated to St. Francis, so that where once the animals ate the hay, now people eat to health of soul and body the flesh of the Lamb without blemish and without spot, our Lord Jesus Christ, who in highest and ineffable love gave himself to us, and lives and reigns with the Father and the Holy Spirit, God eternally glorious, forever and ever. Amen. Alleluia, Alleluia.

—Celano, First Life, 87

December 27

The Daily Humility of God

See, every day he humbles himself as he did when, from his royal throne, he came into the womb of the Virgin; every day he comes to us with the same humility; every day he descends from his Father's bosom into the hands of the priest at the altar.

—Admonition 1

December 28

Who Receives the Body and Blood of the Lord?

The Spirit of the Lord, who dwells in his faithful, is the One who receives the Most Holy Body and Blood of the Lord; all those who do not partake of the same Spirit and presume to receive the Lord, eat and drink to their own judgment (cf. 1 Cr 11:29).

—Admonition 1

December 29

Seeing and Believing

Now as Jesus Christ appeared to his holy Apostles in true flesh, so now he shows himself to us in consecrated bread; and as with their physical sight they saw only his flesh, but contemplating him with the eyes of faith, believed that he was God, so too, now, though we see bread and wine with the eyes of our body, we should see and firmly believe that it is his Most Holy Body and Blood, living and true.

—Admonition 1

December 30

Jesus Our Sacrifice and Oblation

Such was the Father's will that his blessed and glorious Son, whom he gave to us and who was born for us, should through his own blood offer himself on the altar of the cross, a sacrifice and oblation, not for himself through whom all things were made, but for our sins, leaving us an example that we should follow in his footsteps. And the Father wants us all to be saved through him and to receive him with our pure hearts and our chaste bodies. But few are they who do want to receive him and be saved through him, though his yoke is sweet and his burden light.

—Letter to All the Faithful, Second Version

December 31

The Humility of God

Let humanity kneel in fear, let the whole universe tremble, and let heaven rejoice when Christ the Son of the Living God is on the altar in the hands of the priest!

O wonderful ascent, O stupendous descent! O sublime humility! O humble sublimity, that the Lord of the Universe, God and Son of God, should so humbly hide himself, for our salvation, in what seems to be only a small piece of bread! Look, then, upon the humility of God! And pour out your hearts before him. Humble yourselves that he might exhalt you. Hold back nothing of yourselves for yourselves, that he may receive your all who gave his all to you.

—Letter to the Whole Order

The Life of St. Francis:
A Chronology

1182: St. Francis is born in Assisi.

1193: St. Clare is born in Assisi.

1202 (November): Perugia and Assisi are at war. Francis is a prisoner for a year in Perugia.

1204: Francis suffers a long illness.

1204 or early 1205: Francis receives a vision and a message in Spoleto; his conversion begins.

1205 (fall): San Damiano crucifix speaks to Francis: "Go and repair my house, which, as you see, is falling into ruin."

1206 (early): Francis's father takes him before the bishop's court for the return of his money; Francis renounces his father.

1206: Francis nurses lepers in Gubbio.

1206 (summer and fall): Francis returns to Assisi and begins repairs on San Damiano.

1208 (April 16): Bernard of Quintavalle, Peter Catanii, and Giles join Francis.

1208 (summer): Three more brothers join.

1209 (spring): The number of Francis's companions grows to eleven. They go to Rome where Pope Innocent III approves Francis's Rule. The brothers settle at Rivotorto on their return to Assisi.

1209 or 1210: The brothers move to the Portiuncula (St. Mary of the Angels). Possible beginning of the Third Order (Secular Franciscans)

1212 (March 18/19): St. Clare is received at the Portiuncula.

1213–1215: The missionary trips of the brothers. Francis goes to Spain.

1216 (July 16): Pope Innocent III dies. Honorius III succeeds.

1216 (summer): Portiuncula Plenary Indulgence granted by Honorius III.

1219 (May): First Franciscan martyrs leave for Morocco. Francis sails to Damietta in Egypt.

1219 (fall): Francis given an audience by the sultan.

1220: The first Franciscan martyrs are killed in Morocco. Francis goes to the Holy Land.

1220: Peter Catanii is named vicar when Francis resigns.

1221: Peter Catanii dies. Elias named vicar.

1221: Rule of Third Order is approved by Honorius III.

1223 (November 29): Honorius III approves the Rule of St. Francis.

1223 (Christmas): Francis sets up the first Christmas crib for midnight Mass at Greccio.

1224 (August 15–September 29): Francis fasting at La Verna. Receives the stigmata (the wounds of Christ), probably September 14.

1225 (early): Francis returns to Assisi and stays in a hut which Clare has built for him at San Damiano.

1225 (April or May): Francis composes the Canticle of Brother Sun. His eye disease worsens.

1225 (July): Urged by Elias and Cardinal Hugolino (future Gregory IX), Francis goes to Fonte Colombo near Rieti to have his eyes cauterized.

1226 (August–early September): Francis is taken to the bishop's palace in Assisi, his health failing.

1226 (September): Realizing he will die soon, Francis insists on being carried to the Portiuncula. He blesses Assisi.

1226 (October 3): Francis dies at the Portiuncula.

1228 (July 16): Gregory IX canonizes St. Francis.

1253 (August 11): St. Clare dies at San Damiano.

1255 (August 12): Alexander IV canonizes St. Clare.

Writings of St. Francis

Admonitions (undated)

Canticle of Brother Sun (Spring 1225 and October 1226)

Canticle to the Poor Ladies of San Damiano (September 1226)

First and Second Letter to the Custodes (1219)

Form of Life and Last Will for the Poor Ladies (September 1226)

Letter to All the Faithful, 1213–1221 Version, and 1219–1221 Version

Letter to Brother Leo (undated)

Letter to the Clergy (1219)

Letter to a Minister (1221–1223)

Letter to the Rulers of the People (1219)

Letter to St. Anthony (1224)

Letter to the Whole Order (1225–1226)

Office of the Passion (undated)

Paraphrase of the Our Father (undated)

Praises before the Office (undated)

Praises of God—the same parchment (autograph) contains the blessing for Brother Leo (September 1224)

The Prayer Absorbeat (undated)

Rule for Hermitages (1217–1221)

Rule of 1221

Rule of 1223

Salutation of the Virgin Mary (undated)

Salutation of the Virtues (undated)

Song for the Poor Ladies (1225)

The Testament (September 1226)

Medieval Sources Quoted

Anonymous of Perugia (1240)

Legend of Perugia (1246–1247)

Legend of the Three Companions (1305–1320)

Letters of St. Clare to Blessed Agnes of Prague (1234–1253)

Little Flowers of St. Francis (c. 1330)

Lives of St. Francis by Thomas of Celano (1228–1229 and 1246)

Major Life of St. Francis by St. Bonaventure (1263)

Mirror of Perfection (1317–1318)

Process of Canonization of St. Clare (1253)

Rule of St. Clare (August 9, 1253)

Sacrum Commercium, or the Holy Exchange Between St. Francis and His Lady Poverty (1227)

Selected Sermons of St. Bonaventure (1255–1267)

The Testament of St. Clare (undated)

Treatise on the Miracles by Thomas of Celano (1250–1253)

Writings of Leo, Rufino, and Angelo (*I Fiori dei Tre Compagni,* another version of the Legend of Perugia)